How to Succeed in College

HOW TO SUCCEED IN COLLEGE

HERBERT C. GABHART

BROADMAN PRESS
Nashville, Tennessee

ISBN: 0-8054-5066-1
Dewey Decimal Classification: 378
Subject Heading: COLLEGE STUDENTS
Library of Congress Catalog Number: 88-7936

Printed in the United States of America

Library of Congress Cataloging-in-Publication Data

Gabhart, Herbert C., 1914-
  How to succeed in college / Herbert C. Gabhart.
    p.   cm.
  ISBN 0-8054-5066-1
  1. College student orientation—United States.   2. Study, Method
of.   I. Title.
LB2343.32.G3   1989
378'.198'0973—dc19

88-7936
CIP

I dedicate this book, the labors of all who have assisted me in its production, and the sources of all information, ideas, and thoughts which have evolved from my research and experiences through more than a quarter of a century on the campus and in the classroom

TO THAT EVER-EXPANDING HOST OF ENERGET-IC, CAPABLE, WONDERFULLY ENDOWED, AND EXTREMELY FORTUNATE GROUP WHO HAVE THE PRIVILEGE OF PARTICIPATING IN THE COL-LEGE EDUCATIONAL EXPERIMENT.

May their tribe and triumphs increase.

Preface

I have written this book with one very strong conviction in mind. During my twenty-three years as president of Belmont College, I was greatly aware of the need to provide for students some basic orientation for college life, its academic challenges, ways and means of honing personal skills and habits, and ways of taking advantage of the opportunities available in the pursuit of an education. Most students come to college seriously lacking in these. Students could develop academic habits, skills, and competence with a little extra attention given at the right time, in the right way.

What I have written is not a sure cure. It is an attempt to cover most of the areas of weakness, and they are many. I have covered thirty aspects touching those areas. Of necessity, each chapter is brief, merely skeletal, with the hope that some person in an official manner would present the material to the students, enlarging upon the outlines. I have done this for three semesters with a different class each semester. I have found the results rewarding and most helpful to the students according to my observation and the students' own testimonies.

My hope and prayer is that the material could be very helpful to those pursuing education beyond the high-school level. Naturally, I feel that it could also be of value to high-school students. Additionally, I feel the individual student could profit from just reading the material if no teacher were available. At least it could be a good item to distribute to incoming freshmen. It could provide them information and possibly motivation.

Some of the areas I have covered are generally omitted in most of the material now available for orientation purposes.

Herbert C. Gabhart
Nashville, Tennessee

Contents

Introduction

I have seen them come and go by the hundreds for over a quarter of a century . . . college students: freshmen, sophomores, juniors, and seniors. The arrival of the freshmen each fall always created much excitement and joy, but a different excitement and joy from that which surrounded the seniors as they exited at commencement. Both groups faced new worlds to conquer. Neither had all the answers. Both groups thought momentarily they had all the answers, but the freshmen soon began to ask questions while the seniors faced a new set of problems.

It was a big step from the position of a proud high-school senior to that of a lowly freshman in a strange and teeming place. Not many were adequately prepared, possibly not even halfway prepared, for the vastness and variety of the steps just taken and those to be taken. Their grades were acceptable, the IQ and the ACT scores were good enough, but . . .

They were on a different turf now. The air, the sun, and the sky just weren't quite the same. The campus was not like the high-school grounds. It was a community in itself, centered in a forest of buildings and comprised of a rather heterogeneous group ethnically, socially, and spiritually. There was a different life-style. A new era, a new cycle, a new epoch were beginning to unfold. A new way of life had dawned. The faces weren't familiar. The license plates didn't look alike. The evening meal wasn't at the home table. All had changed drastically. There was a new stage on which to perform. The cast was different, the scenes were different, and the acts much longer. The individuals had no lines to memorize—each had to think and act on his or her own.

It was a totally new environment, a small world in itself. New relationships had to be established, new friendships formed.

No wonder many of the freshmen seemed lost, confused, and in a quandary. They had not taken a course in how to become college students. It had not appeared in the high-school curriculum. Orientation to the new way of life and the new responsibilities and opportunities of that life was needed, desperately needed, and in too many cases, sadly lacking.

College life from the first day is too important to be allowed to unravel aimlessly. Too many important things happen during those four years. There is a greater freedom of impulse, greater independence, greater enlightenment of conscience, greater awareness of self, and a greater consciousness in shaping one's own personality. There are the making and fashioning of new friends for a lifetime. Career goals are set; professional training is sought. In many cases, a spouse is chosen and a family begun.

The thrust of this entire book is to provide an awareness, an understanding, and some suggestions on how to cope with the wonderful years of college. No orientation program is a sure cure for that which ails the freshman. None carries a guarantee. None is wholly adequate, but something is far better than nothing.

I offer my "two bits" out of years of experience with the hope and prayer that what I have written will assist, help, encourage, enlighten, and inspire those charged with orienting freshmen, and most of all, that the students themselves will gain from at least a few of the "How To's."

I dare you readers to give it a try.

1
From Home to College

Sometimes it is a long way, mileagewise, or it may be a short distance. In either case it is a far distance from home because once you leave, you cannot really go back. Even if you do go back, it is never the same. It is no longer your primary home.

Leaving home is an extremely important event for the college-bound, sometimes traumatic. Some, however, breathe a sigh of relief and quote the familiar words of the old black spiritual—in a different context, of course—"Free at last! Free at last! Thank God Almighty, I'm free at last." But such instant freedom isn't as grand as expected. Major external supports are severed, and these must be replaced with inner supports. Some depend on external substitutes instead of building inner supports to the left-behind parental authority.

This new freedom carries many personal responsibilities. There is no one to call you each morning, "It's time to get up," no one to lay out clean clothes for the day, and no one to pick up the dirty, discarded ones. New eating habits must be established. The room at college must be kept clean and orderly, and orderliness in the long run is quite a time-saver compared with the time wasted hunting for things and moving them around for convenience.

Newfound freedom brings roommates to get acquainted with, bathrooms to share, space to allocate, schedules to mesh, noise to control, and so forth.

It is quite normal that after a few days the new freedom isn't all glamor as a bit of homesickness sets in. There is a yearning for the old familiar haunts: the private bedroom, home cooking, clean clothes always available, and counsel when needed. Even the presence of sister's nosey cat wouldn't be too bad.

At the same time there is campus homesickness, there is loneliness at home. It is good that you and your parents stay in touch with each other. Write home to share new experiences, not to relive old ones. Look forward to the letters from home for they will be a source of strength and support.

I like very much the advice given by Harry and Bonaro Overstreet in their book, *The Mind Alive:*

> Gradually or abruptly, he must come to the point where he is ready, in a phrase widely used by psychiatrists, to become his own parent. That is, to make for himself decisions previously made for him by an authoritative figure; to organize and direct his own powers, not be merely prodded into their use as a school child is prodded into doing his homework; to accept without self-pity the hazards attendant upon his own free choices; to achieve enough self-respect not to be dependent upon some stronger figure's calling him a good boy; to be a contributor to human welfare, not merely a receiver of bounty; and to replace a boy's will that is "the wind's will" with a man's capacity to make plans and see them through.[1]

It would be quite easy to overindulge such newfound freedom or to play it too safe. Overindulgence will prevent one from accepting responsibility, and playing it safe will allow opportunities to go by. Freedom exploited merely for freedom's sake will produce slavery, causing its victim to be shackled by whims and fantasies that only partially satisfy a carefree, careless existence. Playing freedom too safe produces lack of participation and thereby robs its victim of the glory of struggle and the joy of adjustment to new ventures.

Arriving on campus is a most important event. The physical aspect of the campus is usually impressive. It seems to be a forest of buildings composed of all shapes, sizes, and looks. Some may be quite tall, others sort of round and fat, while others may be "hotel-ish" looking. Each building is an integral part of the whole. There are dormitories, cafeteria, science, humanities, and art buildings. A physical-education building and athletic field will be located usually on the outer rim of the campus. The library is a focal point, almost always centrally located. Many other buildings grace the campus. There are restricted parking lots which you need to become familiar with, as well as sidewalks galore placed for the use of the students rather than the grassy areas. Buildings make a campus physically attractive and provide necessary facilities for the total college experience. They give a sense of continuity and stability to the campus. Get acquainted with the total layout, even the location of the medical facilities.

A college, however, should provide a romantic experience for the students beyond the boy-girl romantic experiences. It is a place to fall in love with new people, new ideas, new concepts, new alternatives, and a place to discover new knowledge. College is a place to learn, and learning should be a self-justifying, self-satisfying experience.

As a freshman, you are immediately confronted with trying to put together all the newfound pieces of the jigsaw puzzle. Here are some of the pieces you will need to put into proper place. After being assigned to your dorm room and becoming acquainted with your roommate, it is wise to unpack and settle in completely. The room may not be what you expected, but it will be adequate for sleeping and studying. Buy your meal ticket or patronize the college cafeteria on an a-la-carte basis. Here again, the food may not be as you like, and I doubt if food at home always pleased you, but most meals are planned with the thought of providing a balanced diet so necessary to good work, both mentally and physcially. Don't live out of fast-food shops, eating hamburgers, french fries, soft drinks, and tomato catsup. Such eating is OK occasionally but inadequate as a steady diet.

You will also want to register as soon as possible and take care of your obligations at the finance office. As soon as you have worked out your class schedule, go immediately to the book store and purchase your textbooks. Be ready to go when the first classroom bell sounds.

Go the second mile in getting acquainted with key people in

your college life: your dorm head resident, your academic counselor, all your professors, student leaders, and the residents on your dorm floor, at least.

I hope you can realize that the campus is more than a place where a few may live in fraternity or sorority houses and go to dances. It is comprised of buildings, people, ideas, schedules, and assignments. It is a place for questioning, not simply a repository of information.

It is not a four-year carnival with midways, sideshows, and Saturday athletic extravaganzas with peanuts, popcorn, and soft drinks. Everything can't always be hilarious and exciting. It is not a perennial three-ring circus—teacher, pupil, and parents. It is not a country club with parties, proms, and picnics. Even though some may enroll simply because of parental insistence, since parents haven't succeeded in being able to corral an impetuous youngster, college is not a correctional institution. It can never be an *in-loco-parentis* place.

So you have arrived at your new home. Make out of it what you will. All the elements are all there for a happy, exciting, and rewarding adventure. You are now a part of the college community. Add your color and flavor to it.

It gives a great feeling to say, "I'm at college now. I look forward to all of the adjustments, opportunities, and responsibilities that arise. I will try to see relevance in a broad education and become acquainted with the changes in civilization mirrored by the institution, my new home."

2
Who Is a College Student?

Now, at least you can say you are an enrollee. But the more sobering question is: "Am I a college student?" As you may guess, the word *student* means a learner, a scholar, one in serious pursuit of knowledge, a seeker of wisdom. Sadly enough, not all who are enrolled in college are in serious pursuit of knowledge. Unfortunately, all entering students do not develop an appetite for learning at the ringing of the classroom bell.

College Is a Place

It is buildings: classrooms, laboratories, library, gymnasium, student center, and dormitories, and so forth. It is people: roommates, fellow dorm residents, professors, fellow students, and administration. It is activities: athletic games, parties, snack-bar conversations, club meetings, church attendance, and dorm meetings. It is work: classroom work, homework, outside work, washing clothes, and cleaning dorm rooms. It is mental work: thinking, listening, reasoning, and evaluating. And in some respects, it is a daily grind.

College is where you must try to get as much as your potential will allow. It is a reservoir of knowledge, a repository of information, an environment of learning.

It is a place away from the routine of life, routine opinions, the tired, prejudiced thought where change is slow. It is a place where you are expected to change, even *required* to change.

College will not give you knowledge, but it will show where knowledge is. It is a place of growing up, finding self, assessing

self, maturing, and learning to accept different persons: their ways
of life, ideas, and habits.

A wag once remarked, "College is a place that's presumed to
mold character, and some of the characters turn out to be very
moldy!" But whose fault is that?

It is quite certain that if you want to be a student, there are
activities and attitudes that must possess you. Negative attitudes
toward certain courses such as mathematics, English, foreign languages, or economics build immediate barriers to learning.

Fortunately, these attitudes can be changed if there is an inspir-
ing teacher or a stimulating classroom climate. It is a tragedy if,
during college days—a period of great physical energy and great
importance, a person spends time in relative idleness and self-
indulgence.

If you seriously want to be a student, it is imperative that you
possess a positive attitude toward learning. The college cannot
trap you and force knowledge down you. It cannot spoon feed all
of its enrollees. It won't wait for you to catch on or catch up.

Various Kinds of College Students

We will start the classification with a group which I call
"sponges." Students in this category try to soak up all the information they can. They would like to be experts on a quiz show. They
are interested in information in capsule form. They are usually
good in rote memory but poor in relationships, evaluation, and
interpretation. Sponges in the material world seldom get involved
in the major aspects of life; usually they are involved in ancillary
things. The capacity of sponges is quite limited.

Another group could be called "parasites." Members of this
group live off of other students' work. They think only what others
think. They have no personal initiative. They also have a tendency
toward cheating, plagiarizing, and leeching on others. They spend
time trying to hang on. They provide no leadership, no new ideas.

There is the "sleeping-beauty" group. As individuals they are
late to class. They doze in class—if not physically, then mentally.
Their minds think back to the evening before, recalling the pleas-

ures of a rock concert or a stint at the movies. They never really wake up to what is going on. Their eyes are too heavy to see the opportunities which abound, and their ears are laden with the carry-over noises of "good times off campus."

The "wise old owl" is both good and bad. This group seems to have superior wisdom and a desire to flaunt it. At times, in their sight, the professor is stale, drab, and flat. Frequently they try to lead him astray, down an alley or avenue of "philosophic thought" that may have no relevance at all to the classroom emphasis or learning process. They think they ought to educate the professors. They revel in wisdom purely for wisdom's sake. This group, however, does have some redeemable traits. Its members are usually well read, good at argumentation, and rather adept at reasoning, even if ambigious or evasive. If they can be kept on track, they are capable of good work.

There is what I choose to call the "squirrel" group. This group spends most of its time gathering "nuts," nuggets of truth, and squirreling them away for a rainy day—examination day, and so forth. After the exam is over all the nuts are gone, and the hoarding place is empty. This group may pass all the tests, sometimes with flying colors, but it has missed out on being able to relate, synchronize, and appropriate the knowledge gained.

The last group I want to mention is the "bee, ant, and beaver" group. You may wonder why I have chosen the ant, the bee and the beaver to represent a group. The ant is a strongly social insect with perfect organization in its communities. It is spoken of in the Bible by the wise man, Solomon, who wrote, "Go to the ant, thou sluggard [sleepy head]; consider her ways, and be wise" (Prov. 6:6). The bee searches far and near for its food to make honey. Isaac Watts wrote, "Little busy bee that improves each shining hour." The beaver is a peaceful, industrious, and ingenious little animal that is always building bridges across streams.

Applying, then, the virtues of two insects and one animal to a group of students, we can describe its members as being willing to spend energy to ferret out new insights, new ideas from far and near. They are able to store this newfound information for later use in building an education experience which could be called a self-satisfying. experience. They have acquired studious habits. They seek to grasp meanings and try to put all the pieces together. They are the winners, the well organized, and the builders.

You as a student must be willing to pay a higher price of personal sacrifice, diligence, and serious commitment to learning. You weren't born a student, but you can become one, hopefully, of the last group.

You are on your own. The terrain is rough; the climb is tough.

Longfellow was right when he wrote in his *Ladder of Saint Augustine.*

> The heights by which great men have reached and kept
> Were not attained by sudden flight,
> But they, while their companions slept,
> Were toiling upward in the night.

Most college students are capable of learning and accomplishing far more than the average contemporary student accomplishes. The time is ideal for self-development mentally, socially, and spiritually, since at college age most young people are fully grown physically. They have great vitality, are usually free from family cares, and very capable of hard work. If these resources are not tapped and fully challenged, laziness may set in and is likely to follow a person throughout life. A good student will give much attention to the development of mental habits, work practices, and time usage.

But believe it or not, it can be most exciting and rewarding because new facts, new ideas, new friends, new challenges, and new goals will provide the thrills and joys of four of the grandest years of your life. Try college; you'll like it.

Wherever students are together in conversation, in the dormitories, in the classroom, at the cafeteria table and at social gatherings, learning experiences are sure to transpire. Stay alert!

3
Getting the Most from College

Introduction

If you want to know the answer to that question, you are asking a serious, important one.

There are two obvious reasons why: first, the very heart of an educational experience should coincide with the intrinsic meaning of the word *education*. It comes from the Latin word *educatus* which means "to lead out," to lead out of the past, to lead out into new vistas of knowledge with new experiences, and to experience new ideas. Second, the cost of a four-year college education is in the range of twenty-five to forty thousand dollars, quite an investment of time and money and in most cases a sacrifice on the part of both parents and student. A secondary question is, Is a college education worth such an investment?

Simply by way of illustration, take the figure of thirty thousand dollars as the cost of a four-year college education. That amount of money invested at 10 percent compounded annual interest would amount to approximately half a *million* dollars at the end of forty years. Just to digress for a moment: Dr. Albert Einstein was once asked to name the most important discovery ever made by man. His answer was quite interesting and simple—compound interest.

Can it be proven or expected that a four-year educational experience would be a better investment of thirty thousand dollars?

We have said too many years that a college degree is worth at least a hundred thousand dollars more to the recipient than if no degree had been achieved. On today's market we haven't updated that figure. Think of this. I believe the records will show that a college degree-holding person will earn on an average at least ten thousand dollars more per year than a nongraduate. If that is true, then ten thousand dollars a year compounded at 10 percent interest would be worth approximately two million dollars at the end of forty years. Is such an educational experience really worth it? Yes, and there is so much more to it than just money.

If I have made you think enough about the possible worth of such an educational experience, let me offer some suggestions about how to develop the potential in such an experience. Here are four good suggestions by Bell, Burhardt, and Lawhead from their book *Introduction to College Life:*

> 1. The relationship of good reading skills to success in college is primary.
> 2. A second skill, valuable if not actually necessary for reasonable success in college, is the ability to listen constructively . . . But listening, although students engage in it for a good part of their time, is hopelessly neglected as a particular skill requiring systematic and controlled practice.
> 3. Another important aspect of college readiness is the skill of candid, dispassionate, objective thinking. Good thought, like good reading, demands a sharp distinction between what is important and what is relatively unimportant.
> 4. What are the attitudes which block successful and satisfying completion of the freshman year? The obstacles all revolve around the central pole of self-consciousness. Fear, anxiety, selfishness, aggressiveness, timidity, lethargy—these often spring from unwholesome conceptions of the relationship between self and society.[1]

Now, I want to offer you eight additional suggestions of my own:

1. You must invent disciplines to keep the deeper levels of energy within reach. There is more than one level of energy just as there is what is known to an athlete as "second and third wind."

In order to tap a new level of energy, push right through the obstruction of fatigue. Fatigue is not the end of your supply of energy. It may be nothing more than a suggestion to shift gears in order to scale the incline. New levels of energy are tapped when you throw your will into the saddle. A good thing to practice is to give your word of honor to yourself like saying, "I will not stop short of anything less than my best." This will require the adoption of a high goal, the acceptance of a severe challenge, and the application of midnight oil. The goal, the challenge, and the midnight oil will force upon you a category of priorities. Frivolity, foolishness, and fiddling around must be stifled.

2. You must develop proper motives, which are powerful ingredients in efficient performance. Excellence is never thrust upon the individual. Motives come from conviction, ideals, and desires. You must answer the question: Who am I? Your answer must be either a redeemed child of God with limitless potential, or a physical being with an insatiable materialistic appetite. If you accept the first, that of a child of God, then your motives will be to honor Him and develop your God-given abilities to the fullest. If the latter, then your motives will be selfishness and greed, passion and pleasure.

There is a second question thrust upon you: What is my place in life? Here again the answer is twofold: to get or to give. If your place in life is to get, then your motives will be pitched in the direction of a "quick buck" and an easy road. If your purpose in life is to give, then you will not hesitate to prepare to the fullest at any cost in order that the quality and quantity of the gift of yourself will be meaningful and uplifting to society. A third question comes to you: How am I to do that which I must do? There is no excelling without tremendous labor. There are no shortcuts, no easy roads, other than those that lead downward.

3. You must create incitements to be good and to do good work. College is an exciting time, but excitements do not necessarily incite one to do good. The discovery of a new word with all of its meaning and usages lends itself to a most thrilling adventure in conversation and writing. Words that come to you in the study

of a new course should stimulate you to probe deeper and wider. Train your ears to hear the words and your mind to bring up the proper mental picture. This will whet your appetite for additional company with strange, new words.

The very thought of a new course of study should cause you tremendous concern and joy. The privilege of having new areas opened and new truths to break in upon your mind and heart should incite you to action, like the taking of a trip to some unknown but desirable island. For instance, the study of chemistry will open to you a museum of artifacts, a storeroom of useful knowledge, and an understanding of many of nature's beautiful secrets.

New words, new courses, and new opportunities should remove forever the routine and doldrum of mediocre living. Add to this the fact that a book is a new book until you have read it, and you will find the library a place of new thrills, joys, and adventures.

4. Somehow you must acquire the magic of eagerness and enthusiasm rather than allowing yourself to become apathetic.

Let me contrast the eager student with the apathetic student. An eager student will meet the teacher halfway—all the way if necessary—while the apathetic student demands that the teacher meet him. The eager student will seek out new situations to learn while the apathetic student will use every means of escape in order to avoid learning. In fact, the teacher must block all exits and trap the student for him to learn even enough to get by and continue to trek through the halls of learning. The eager student will joyfully handle all assignments without criticism or feeling of being overworked while the lazy, apathetic one will complain and murmur about normal work being overwork.

If you lose your enthusiasm, you have lost one of life's greatest producers of energy. Fatigue has a way of vanishing in the presence of eagerness and enthusiasm. Let me throw in right here a truth which I hope you will long remember: no one likes a negative, passive personality. If you want friends, cultivate an enthusiastic personality.

5. Take time to sit yourself down around a conference table

where your many selves are assembled and decide right now which one of the many selves will be chairperson of the board. You will never attend a more important meeting. And once the chairperson has been elected, respect him or her and abide by his official decisions.

You are a composite of many selves. There is the self of passion, and many times you will be pressured by your cohorts to yield and follow some passionate desire. You must not do this. There is the self of pleasure, which will knock constantly at your heart. Many attractive occasions will clamor for attention and support. Some of them will be most worthwhile and acceptable, but here again you must seek the advice of the chairperson of the board.

6. Be sure to keep an open mind. An open mind is more than a tunnel through which a swift breeze may pass unobstructed. But keep an open mind as a depository for ideas, experiences, and facts. It is more than stuffing the memory. It is most difficult to open a closed mind, and, remember, you do not have to open your mouth to have an open mind.

7. Be very inquisitive. Ask questions. You will receive more from asking more. Ask how, why, where, and to what extent. Ask, ask, ask. Most professors have far more knowledge than classroom time will allow them to expound. Ask yourself questions, such as: Do I understand this? Have I researched the problem or the topic adequately? Have I dealt with the heart of the matter?

8. Profit from your own mistakes and the mistakes of others, for you won't live long enough to make them all yourself. Learn by observation and application. Try not to make the same mistake twice.

The following chapters will be most helpful to you as I will offer suggestions and ways and means of improvement at various levels and approaches to a full educational experience.

4
Starting Right

Introduction

The way you *start* your educational career at this point could be as valuable as the way you finish. The first week may well be more important than the last week, which is usually one of celebration. The first week gets you started right: in the right direction with the right habits and schedules. In fact, if you don't get started right, you may not survive until the finish.

You have paid your entrance fee for the privilege to attack the four-year educational course before you, so plan carefully from the start. Your first week is quite crucial.

You will be on a fast track, a different track for you, not at all like that in high school or the marketplace if you have been out there working for a few years. As you run your educational race, it will not be a relay where you can pass off the baton to another. It is all your race.

A little boy made a mad dash to catch his bus. He missed it by a few seconds. An onlooker exclaimed, "Well, fellow, if you'd have run faster you would've made it!"

"No, sir, I ran fast enough. I just didn't start in time."

And believe me, that is a parable of how and when to start.

Be sure to start on the right path. You don't want to be a "Wrong-way Corrigan" who flew the wrong way, or a Roy Riegels who ran the football in the wrong direction on the afternoon of January 1, 1929, at the Rose Bowl between Georgia Tech and California. Riegels was the center on the California team and as the ball squirted out of the hands of Thomason of Tech, it fell into the hands of Riegels. In the confusion he ran in the wrong direction, only to be tackled by a teammate at the one-yard line. A moment later Tech blocked a kick getting two points that gave Tech an 8 to 7 victory.

The right direction: start with positive mental attitudes. In the next chapter we will consider how to develop and maintain positive mental attitudes, but without being repetitious, let me state that it is desirable to have a good attitude about the educational institution to become your alma mater. You must have had solid reasons for selecting it. Be proud of your college. You are a part of it.

The administration of the institution is not an adversary. It functions to provide facilities, faculty, and a fine climate for learning. Your tuition and fees will build no buildings and provide few, if any, facilities other than a few laboratory items and a few library books. The administration must raise the funds to provide the facilities.

Your professors are not your adversaries. They are not out to flunk you. They are your advocates. They want you to learn; they are willing to help you learn; they are capable of helping you and few of them, if any, have favorites in their classes. Get acquainted with your teachers immediately. You are on an equal level with everyone else.

Approach every class session with enthusiasm and excitement. If you are prepared, you will more than likely look forward to what will develop during the class session, but if unprepared, you will look constantly at your watch, hoping for the time to race by before being called on to recite.

The privilege to study is indeed a rare privilege. Your study will be planned out by your professor, and there will be rhyme and reason to these plans and assignments. In one respect, your professors are your personal intellectual coaches. You will have not just one coach but several who are knowledgeable in their areas of competence. Take their counsel, direction, and suggestions.

Adopt workable daily procedures. Do this happily and voluntarily, even by force if necessary, for habits early formed are so basic. Respect and honor those worthwhile habits until the habits become second nature. Ninety-five percent of our behavior, feeling, and response is habitual. The pianist does not decide which keys to strike. The dancer does not stop to consider which foot to move where. The response is automatic. It will take discipline and careful self-assertiveness. The worst boss anyone can have is a bad habit, for habits are either the best of servants or the worst of masters.

I counsel you to work very hard at forming good habits, so they will become as hard to break as bad ones. You will not form good habits instantly. Each day you will weave a thread of it until the cable becomes hard to break, adequate to sustain you.

Prepare for the first official day. Get your textbooks and have them with you as you enter your first classroom. Read the biography regarding the author. Study the introduction to the textbook and try to sense the purpose given and the direction the author is taking.

Look over the course description in your catalog and let that always be in the background of your mind.

Become very familiar with the campus. Walk over it before your classes begin so you know where each class will meet. Know the building, classroom number, and floor where the class is located. Time yourself from one building to another. This will provide relaxed going to and from buildings rather than the necessity to make mad dashes. It might sound like a chore, but if you work with patience and consistent effort, you will find it all so pleasurable.

Be on time at the starting gate. Be there. Come out of the starting post at the sound of the bell. A later start will produce a late finish. As you arrive at the starting gate have your lesson well prepared. Most assignments can be handled on a day-to-day basis *but if one gets behind it is most difficult to catch up.* Cramming during the last week of the semester just won't cut it.

Listen carefully to the first remarks made by the professor. Get plenty of sleep in your bedroom and not while in class. As you sit down, tune in your ears. Tune out memories of other things. Concentration is necessary and rewarding. Just as most professors enjoy hearing themselves deliver their lectures, they equally enjoy and appreciate their students listening most carefully. The classroom is not a place for conversation unless directed by the professor. Make readable, logical notes.

Size up your professor. Observe his or her method and manner of delivery. Look for those things which are stressed as being most central. This is far better than trying to practice "apple polishing" which tends to backlash. Your professor has the red pencil: don't ever forget that.

Practice reviewing the previous day's classroom lecture, assignment, discussion and notes. Relate them to today's assignment. This will provide continuity and project an awareness of the major thrust of the course.

Work first and play later. It is true that "all work and no play may make Jack a dull boy," but all play and no work will make Jack a much duller boy. It is essential that you give your physical body attention. Physical exercise will tend to improve your mental acuity, that is, if not overdone to the extent that the body is too tired to provide energy for the mind.

You will enjoy your social life much better if you can participate in various activities, knowing you have not neglected your assignments or worrying about when you will have time to do the necessary preparation.

You have twenty-four hours a day. A wise schedule made and followed should allow enough time for all of the important, relevant matters.

So get started right. *Stay caught up, stay on schedule.* Respect those viable habits, knowing that the more you practice them the better you become at them. You have your newfound freedom.

You are on your own. It isn't wise to goof off the first week, thinking it is not very important. The fact is: *it is most important.*

If you were running a hundred-yard dash, it would be far better to get a good start at the beginning. You can get this in your studies!

5
How to Develop and Maintain a Positive Attitude

Introduction

It is not trite to say that your attitude will determine your altitude. "Pardon me, your attitude is showing." We really see things as we wish, and what we see sharply determines our attitude: positive or negative.

The giant Goliath had Israel's army in a fearful stand-off position. Young David had arrived behind the lines of the Israelites with food for his brothers. He heard the taunts of the giant and saw the defeatist attitude of the people. Notice David's response that has been described in this manner: when David saw the giant he heard the Israelites say, "He is so big we can't do anything with him," while David said, "He is so big I can't miss him!" What a difference in attitude! Our big problem is trying to find out what caused the difference.

Establishing Some Good Intellectual Attitudes

Regarding Professors

The relationship between a student and teacher is vitally important. A professor constantly tries to open windows with good intellectual insights for the students to grapple with. The professor is a good shepherd trying to lead his sheep into green pastures.

I can recall that during my educational preparation days I learned far more from the professors I knew best and respected greatly. The harder they were, the more I learned. The more I now appreciate their memory. I had very positive feelings about them.

I admired their knowledge and skill in handling knowledge. I sensed their eagerness to share with the class. I never felt they enjoyed making it hard on us. Even though at times I felt less positive than at others, I never lost a definitely positive feeling regarding them. Following their instructions and responding to their challenges were like exploring a cave.

I admit there were times when there seemed to be a dissonance between the professors' instruction to the students to think for themselves and the students' necessity to memorize the teachers' lectures and give them back at examination time. But such dissonance and disparity are always a part of any learning experience. The professor's aim, purpose, and direction were sufficient to keep the attitude on a positive level.

Regarding Assignments

Classroom assignments frequently evoke from the students negative reactions such as, "too long," "too short a period for preparation," and, "too much other work to do." If, on the other hand, you look upon learning as panning for gold and not trivial pursuit, then the negative melts away, and the positive attitude takes over. A jaunt to the library to look up additional material is like taking a trip through a museum. Completing written assignments should be viewed as scaling mountain peaks in order to obtain a fuller and clearer view of the larger horizon. Each assignment then will produce an anxiety about what is on the next page, what is the next new idea or new thought. Doing homework could be likened to clearing new ground, preparing to consume a good meal, or uncovering some valuables.

Regarding Various Disciplines of Study

Some students have negative reactions and attitudes toward subjects they do not like such as mathematics, science, English, modern languages, and so forth. But these reactions can be dispelled and replaced with positive attitudes. Learning is not a case of likes and dislikes. A good teacher can change the attitude of students, especially if the lectures are stimulating, exciting, and understandable.

Literature which to some might be on the no-no side of the ledger can be made most interesting and desirable. Literature introduces one to the best thoughts of yesteryears, the charming personalities of bygone days, and provides a wealth of inspiration.

Science to some has been lackluster, but now it is revealing and producing amazing knowledge for us to live with.

History, to many dull and irrelevant, has become one of the best sources of understanding the world situation today. My major professor constantly reminded us that one never understands anything until it is understood historically. History does more than tell us when and where the Pilgrims landed on American soil. It tells us *why* they came here. One lesson to be learned from history is that there was only one indispensable man: Adam.

Take the study of modern languages—French, for example. Studying French can become like a tour of France with an introduction to French life, culture, and history. It is mostly a matter of how we view our studies—attitude.

Regarding Routines, Schedules and Requirements

Some of these strike us at times as rather tedious and obnoxious, but wait a minute. Routines, schedules, and requirements are for the good of the group. Everyone can't follow the policy of doing as one pleases. That would be anarchy, confusion, and conflicts. Parking regulations are for the convenience and good of the larger group. There must be restricted zones. Everyone can't park at the front door. Dorm life must have some semblance of order and understanding. Noises must be curbed, cleanliness upheld, and hours respected. In some institutions chapel attendance is required. When viewed properly, it can be one of the most worthwhile gatherings of the week and the only time for the educational community to get together.

Regarding the New Heterogenous Community

An educational institution's population is a microcosm of the world. Different ethnic groups, individuals from different cultures and backgrounds, add to the charm and fascination of the new community life. Each group must learn to appreciate the other; each should strive to understand the other.

Hindrances to Building a Positive Mental Attitude

A fixed mind-set birthed by tradition, prejudices, and misunderstanding can thwart an effort to be positive. Some students give the impression: "I am neither for nor against apathy!" Or, "lasso me if you can and stuff me with 'learning.' " All such attitudes are fatal to positive thinking.

Some live in a world of impossibilities. The thought of impossibility tends to create impossibility. Transfer such a negative feeling to the realm of a challenge by reacting to it aggressively and positively. Sort of develop the habit and attitude that if a thing is difficult or impossible, then do it or bust. Regardless, the effort is worth it.

So you have a problem. Great. So does everyone else. Helen Keller, (if you don't know who she was, I dare you to look this up) once said, "Keep your face to the sunrise, and you cannot see your shadow." Problems are pregnant with opportunities. Look at the problem until you find the opportunities.

Don't go to sleep at night with your head loaded with worries and unpleasant thoughts, but rather fill your heart with gratitude. While the mind and body are at rest, let them be revitalized with energy-building thoughts and not the contrary.

Don't expect to build a positive attitude all at once. Don't expect an instantaneous miracle. You won't be able to build one reciting mumbo-jumbo platitudes such as: "Think big, think mink, forget the rabbit habit," or "when the going gets tough, the tough get going." Playing it "cool" won't produce either. Playing it cool is an evasion of life. Keep up with the struggle!

How, then, can one maintain a positive mental attitude? Here are six suggestions:

1. *Think positively.* Aspire to be more than average, for *average* has been defined as "the worst of the best and the best of the worst." This is a better world than many think. It is a terrific opportunity to have the privilege of attending a fine educational institution with freedom of speech and resources available.

2. *Work happily and live cheerfully.* You must make your own happiness. It is not from outside but from inside. Try to have joy in your work. If you lose an eye and it is replaced with a glass eye, demand that the glass eye have a twinkle in it.

3. *Reflect clearly and objectively.* Look at everything carefully and objectively. Remember that no responsibility or task is more than a series of little ones, any one of which you can do, taken one at a time.

4. *Live gratefully.* Think of what it is costing to pay your bills. Think of what others have done to make the educational buildings possible, of all of the opportunities that surround you, think of the benefits that have come from the past, and of what this age has inherited from previous cultures.

5. *Believe sincerely.* Believe in yourself and in the institution, in the educational system of which you are a part, in your beliefs. Doubt your doubts, or sooner or later you will believe your doubts and doubt your beliefs. Have faith in yourself, in your colleagues, your professors, and your goals.

6. *Strive to develop the power of the positive no.* This will help from being divided within. Stand by your convictions, your fundamental moral virtues with a positive no! when the situation demands. Employ courage and fortitude. In this manner you will stamp out softness, lethargy, and indifference, all enemies to a positive mental attitude.

6
Staying Alive-eyed

Introduction

I hope you won't think this chapter is too much of a digression at this point. It may not be as practical as our other subjects, for as you read it you might get the impression of an editorial vignette. I am trying to say, "You must stay alert to stay alive," not a life-or-death situation but the difference between living and merely existing.

We are a generation of watchers and listeners, not seers. We watch television. We listen to the radio and records, but we move at such a fast clip that we don't see much flying through the air, gliding down the interstate, or reclining in a chaise lounge. Even if we are devotees to the computer, we can't see everything looking at the computer screen.

Alive-eyed means to be observant, discerning, and attentive. The word *behold* conveys some of the idea. It carries the idea of wonder, thrill, joy, admiration, and most of all surprise. Our eyes usher concepts to our minds for interpretation and meaning. Entrepreneurs see more than the commonplace. Discoverers look deeper and farther than the average. Scholars search far and near for new truths. Alive-eyed, then, may convey the idea of being eagle-eyed, hawk-eyed, cat-eyed, and Argus-eyed. The eagle can see great distances; the hawk surveys the immediate surroundings; the cat can prowl through the darkness. Argus was a character in Greek mythology with a thousand eyes.

Without being too simplistic I would suggest that if you wish to become alive-eyed, you must learn to *look:* look up, look down, look out, look in, look around, and look through.

Learn to look up. There are fewer objects to obstruct your vision as you look up. No one knows how high is up. The majesty and magnitude of the earth and sky become apparent. Visions are born while looking up. The feeling of awe and wonder brings the assurance that there is more, much more, area yet unplumbed. In a world of confusion and disarray one can, by looking up, read the regular and precise movements of the heavenly bodies and realize that such actions are not fazed or troubled by the world's struggles, and that time marches on.

Learn to look down. One might become a bit dizzy trying to look up all the time. The major activities of life occur in a space no more than fifteen to twenty feet high. Christopher Columbus, who is credited with discovering America, practiced the art of looking down. One day on the shores of Genoa, Italy, Columbus saw a seed which his mind told him came from another place. The mighty, restless ocean had swept it to the shores of Italy. With his mind seeking the answer, his soul caught a vision. The rest of the story you know. There is much to see by looking down occasionally. By turning over some rocks or shuffling the leaves around, you may see something never seen before. You may come to a renewed appreciation of the miracles of the earth and thereby get a vision that will bless humankind.

Learn to look out. A philosopher once remarked that human beings live in prison cells with the walls lined with mirrors and can see only themselves. How pathetic. Before you are imprisoned by self, look out and see a world of people, over five billion. Many are hungry, suffering, dying and in need of opportunities for self-improvement. Look out more and look less into the mirror. Rest your eyes. Listen to the call of the distant. Find a way to build a bridge. See opportunities shaping up. Seize the moment lest it slip away. Look, listen, and act. People are huddled in masses, marching in droves, and cringing in hunger and fear. Find a way to help; search for solutions; stay alive-eyed.

Learn to look in. Introspection is very good but not good all the time. You need to know what is inside of yourself: your desires, motives, and goals. But I am thinking more about looking into new areas, the unentered rooms of life, the undiscovered. Life has been likened to a corridor with many doors, many of the doors yet unopened. You would do well to make haste to open as many as you can before the ultimate one opens. Search out ancillary avenues of knowledge that will shed some light upon your major interest. Visit museums, art galleries, libraries, and historical places.

Learn to look around. I remember reading once about what group of sparrows did when a loaf of bread fell from a delivery truck. As the bread hit the hard pavement crumbs broke from the loaf which rolled to one side. The sparrows fought each other for the crumbs while the loaf remained unnoticed. Finally, one alive-eyed little bird discovered the loaf by looking around. A parallel to this comes from a classroom experience in a university as "a group of students were discussing important issues with the professor of mathematics. As the group broke up the professor said, 'Any way you must play the game of life.' "

"But, professor, how are we to play the game of life when we don't know where the goal posts are?" asked one alive-eyed student.[1] You must stay alert to the eternal realities of life to know where the goal posts are.

Learn to look through. By looking through the real we might see the unreal, the invisible. Could we have discovered the laws of the universe if we had neglected to see the laws in operation in objects with which we were familiar? Learn to see the realities which the eye may sometimes miss. Familiarity with what is seen may suggest or imply something yet unseen.

There appear to be at least six areas in which we must continue to receive if we are to remain vitally alive in mind and emotion:[1]

1. To begin, then, almost at random, we have to receive into ourselves the riches of the human tradition. In a good home, the child starts becoming acquainted with these very early: in poem, song, story, and in simple rules of courtesy and cooperation.

2. We have to receive into ourselves the experience of many other people. Baudelaire defined the poet as a person uniquely able 'to be at once himself and every man.'

3. In the third place, we have to go on receiving the type of information that will keep us growing in our own special line of work.

4. Once more—and this often comes hard for us—we have to remain open to facts that challenge our own preconceptions, misconceptions, and prejudices . . .

5. Again, in order that we may not live as emotional strangers on the planet that is our home, we must continuously receive what the natural world has to give through its sights and sounds, its color and form, its mind-stretching spaces, and its incredibly intricate detail . . .

6. Our final necessity is closely related to this one: as long as we live, if we are to be alive in mind as well as body, we must willingly receive into consciousness questions about humanity and the universe that have as yet no conclusive answers.[2]

I suggest also that you try to greet each morning bright-eyed, having gotten adequate sleep. The late-night pizza may not be as important to your good health as the sleep lost in going for the pizza. Stay in good health. A tired body is not ideal for an alive-eyed condition.

Stay alert physically to be alive-eyed mentally. It will pay rich dividends.

7
Increasing Reading Skills

Introduction

This subject may seem a bit misplaced addressed to students in one of the most literate countries on the face of the earth, but don't be too hasty. Our college students have been referred to as "reading cripples," many of whom do not read any better than those on the eighth-grade level. Why is this true?

Some educators have estimated that more than half of school failures are due to poor reading. What can be done about this?

I feel very strongly that proper emphasis has not been given to reading. We have assumed that since young people learn to read early in their educational days the job has been accomplished, and each person will improve as maturity sets in.

Kind of Readers

There are at least four kinds of readers.

Those who read only for pleasure. When this is the case, little concern is given to increasing the speed of reading since, after all, it is for pleasure. There is little concern for retention of what is read. These are those who read the mystery stories, novels, and so forth.

Those who read to learn. Reading to them is a source of knowledge. They read books related to their profession in order to stay up to date. They read trade journals, daily newspapers, periodicals, and the like. Reading is vital to them.

Those who read for escape. To many it is a way of clearing the mind of the day's activities and thus a way of preparing for retiring at night. To others it is a means of escape from the responsibilities and duties of life.

Those who consider reading an ingenious device for avoiding thought.

The Value in Reading

It is obvious that people should read. We have two eyes and one tongue.

Edward Gibbon wrote in his *Memoirs,* "My early and invincible love of reading . . . I would not exchange for the treasures of India."

William Godwin put it like this, "He that loves reading, has everything within his reach. He has but to desire, and he may possess himself of every species of wisdom to judge and power to perform."

The Bible has the older man Paul urging his young friend Timothy to "give attendance to reading" (1 Tim. 4:13).

> Some books are to be tasted, others to be swallowed, and some few to be chewed and digested; that is, some books are to be read only in parts; others to be read, but not curiously; and some few to be read wholly, and with diligence and attention. Some books also may be read by deputy, and extracts made of them by others; but that would be only in the less important arguments, and the meaner sort of books; else distilled books are like common distilled waters, flashy things. Reading maketh a full man; conference a ready man; and writing an exact man. And therefore, if a man write little, he had need [sic] have a great memory; if he confer little, he had need have a present wit; and if he read little, had had need have much cunning, to seem to know that he doth not. Histories make men wise; poets witty; the mathematics subtile; natural philosophy deep; moral grave; logic and rhetoric able to contend.[1]

Ways of Reading

A wag once remarked, "The way to read a book is to take a

knife and cut through the pages, then smell the knife and if the smell is OK, proceed to read the book."

You may approach reading in several ways.

Glance over the pages to gain an overview. This will help you to focus on the parts most relevant to your needs or wishes.

Survey the pages in order to spot key words, key thoughts, and the emphasis of the writer.

Read the first sentence of each paragraph in order to get the drift of the writing. In this manner you can be more selective.

Read each word very carefully due to the importance of what is being read. This can be very time consuming and in most cases not totally necessary.

Some Hindrances to Good Reading

It is bad to vocalize words in reading. Moving the lips consumes time and energy. This habit is almost equal to reading aloud which not only slows the reading process tremendously, but slows the the absorption of meaning. Too, the eyes tend to get ahead of the voice.

Choose a favorable reading environment so you may not be easily distracted. Radios, television sets, nearby conversation, and other noices will hamper your reading.

Be sure to have good light, a well-ventilated room, and a comfortable chair, but not too comfortable because sleep may result.

Lack of concentration, or mind wandering, can become quite a hindrance. Not all reading material immediately captures the mind and holds it. You will need to force your mind to hang in there. You cannot think of other things while reading. Do not have a split mind.

How to Improve Your Reading and Your Reading Speed

Increase your eye span by letting it include more than one word. Let it encompass phrases and thought patterns, not words, Practice this by marking off some paragraph and going over it time and time again.

Practice daily reading more quickly, even if at first you may sacrifice comprehension and retention. This is the same as pushing yourself in a race. A racer will never learn to run faster just by jogging casually. Push, push, push.

Try to reduce fixation of eyes per line by lengthening the eye sweep. Keep going in order to avoid regressions of the eyes to something previously covered.

Try to achieve a rhythm in your reading. Avoid rushes followed by sudden stops.

Concentration is most vital just as lack of concentration is a serious hindrance. Practice, practice. Read, read, read.

Read the following three times.

First, read it as you normally read.	Time _____.
Second, mark it into phrases and read.	Time _____.
Third, push yourself to your limit.	Time _____.

Anyone viewing Earth as a complex integrated whole—the view that Space travel gives—can see that water is now one of our planet's major problems. We can use spacecraft to help solve the problem, as will appear in a moment.

An observer in earth orbit need not be an expert to perceive that some huge basins and plains are producing little because they lack water. He can see 18,000 miles of Earth's coastlines virtually uninhabited for the same reason, although oceans lap at their shores. He will find farms abandoned in many areas because pumping has exhausted the underground water. Wherever he looks on the globe, he will notice growths of "urban sprawl" that require more and more water for the hordes of newcomers swarming into the human hives.

Man now faces a serious, worldwide shortage of water amid plenty. There are 326 million cubic miles of water on the planet—about 1,100 billion gallons. This would be more than ample for everyone, if it were all fit for use. But 97 percent of it is in the oceans, too salty for drinking or irrigation. Another 2 percent is locked in ice caps and glaciers, frozen and unusable. The tiny useful fraction that is left is neither evenly distributed, properly used, nor prudently safeguarded. Even where it is abundant, man is making it unusable by carelessly poisoning it.[2]

How to Mark a Book You are Reading

Reading at times requires reading between the lines. Comprehension and retention of what you read may require marking between the lines.

Underline an important word, line, or thought. Follow this with vertical lines in the margins to emphasize the statement already underlined. You may wish to use double lines in underlining if you consider that portion of special interest.

Place a star or an asterisk either in the margin or at the point in the paragraph which you wish to emphasize. Do not do this too frequently since too many stars or asterisks will clutter your intentions.

Place sequential numbers, ideas, or thoughts in the margin so you can follow easily and logically.

Circle words or figures that are important. This makes the words and figures stand out.

Write relevant comments or questions in the margin or at the bottom of the page. If you question an idea or figure, place a question mark in the margin.

If your filing system is minimal, record the page numbers containing ideas or information on the inside back cover for easy reference through the years.

If an idea or thought connects with something similar in other books, put a reference to other books in the margin, just opposite that idea or thought.

Don't hesitate to mark your books. They are your tools. Keep them sharp. There is no need to read an entire book the second time to find something you want. Just be sure to know what marking system you are following and do not mark haphazardly and carelessly.

8
How to Listen

Introduction

Listening is an art, a fine art. We have one mouth and two ears, and we should take a tip from nature: the mouth is made to close, but the ears aren't. If you are talking, you aren't listening.

I got my interest in listening sharpened and spurred when Wallace Johnson, co-founder of one of the largest hotel/motel chains in the world, suggested to me that we should offer a course in listening at the college. He told of countless experiences in dealing with executives and employees who had not learned to listen.

The popularity of the CB car radio underscored the practice of listening: "Silver Eagle, do you have your ears on?" Have our ears been the "neglected child"?

We listen more than any other activity except breathing. Statistics have been released indicating that an average day we spend time like this:

- 9 percent writing
- 16 percent reading
- 30 percent talking
- 45 percent listening (but how well do we listen?)

American Airlines, on one of its flights, announced the name of the pilot, and only one out of a hundred remembered the name.

Have we spoon-fed our youngsters in school and not required them to listen by constantly repeating and then eventually handing out memos?

Ford Motor Company has a slogan: "We listen better."
The 3M Company says: "We hear you."
How about pondering the poem of the wise old owl:

> The wise old owl sat on an oak;
> The more he saw the less he spoke;
> The less he spoke the more he heard;
> Why aren't we like that wise old bird?[1]

Hindrances to Good Listening

Lack of purpose. You might ask "Why listen? I can find out what I need when I need it."

Jumping to conclusions. "There is no need to listen any longer. I know where this is coming out. It is obvious."

Preoccupation. The speaker may be slightly interesting or the reading material of some value, but the mind is occupied with other matters. It is impossible to think about one thing and listen to something entirely different.

Wandering eyes. It is difficult to hear what is being said if our eyes are freewheeling, taking in all the surroundings.

Impatience. Have you felt like saying, "Hurry up. I have other things to do. Don't be tedious. I've got to go"?

Slouchiness. I have seen some students sprawl in chairs, casting their eyes at the teacher as if to say, "I dare you to get my attention, and if you should for a moment, you won't hold it for any length of time."

Dislike of speaker or teacher. Maybe something about the performer strikes you unfavorably. You don't like the attire, the voice, or the mannerisms.

Daydreaming. It's a good thing if it is done at the proper time, but not as a competitor to good listening.

Doodling. Doodling and drawing artistic doodads is a severe hindrance to good listening. It splits attention.

Faking attention. Some people are marvelous actors, good fakers. They appear to be pious listeners but are nothing but "put ons."

It is difficult to listen, but it is difficult to know if one is listening. It is easy to know if one is speaking. The voice can be heard, but no one can detect the acuity of listening.

Types of Listening

There is an inner voice in each one of us that should be listened to. It may be the voice of conscience. It may be the spirit of achievement. It may be one's own best self. It may be intuition or the restless pulse of care. Most of us talk to ourselves, and we need to listen to ourselves.

We need receptive ears to listen to others. Our friends need our ears and our empathy. Our teachers want us to listen, else their lectures are in vain and their words fall upon barren soil. We need the counsel and advice of others. To become good followers we need to listen to our leaders. To become good leaders we need to listen to our followers. Employees need to listen to the employers, and employers need to listen to the employees. Students need to listen to teachers, and vice versa.

Thus, to listen well one should have receptive ears, a receptive heart, and a receptive soul. We are far more capable of listening than we practice. The average person in listening uses only about 25 percent of his native ability. Sixty percent of our misunderstanding comes from poor listening while only one percent is chargeable to poor communications. Unbelievable!

How to Tune In and Tune Up Our Listening Capabilities

First of all, have a hearing checkup to be sure there is nothing wrong with your hearing. There should be no organic impediment interfering with your hearing capability.

Sit at attention and pay attention. Look the professor in the eye. Overlook any voice quality defect or mannerism. Focus on what is being said. Keep on maintaining eye contact.

Perk up. Keep alert. Don't let drowsiness overtake you. When you feel it coming on, breathe deeply, and just sit that much taller. Remember, a sleepy head contains a sleepy mind.

Tune-up. Tune up your mind as you would tune up your violin or any other instrument. Get in tune with the speaker, the professor. Avoid being in another country on a different safari.

Jot it down. As you listen jot down things of interest and of importance. Reflect upon what you have jotted down and review the notes for permanent filing in your mind. Evaluate what is being said.

It is not too harsh to say, "Shut up." Be sure you aren't competing with the one speaking. Don't try to upstage your speaker. Listen; don't show off.

Ask questions. This involves you with what is being said. It accentuates your motive in listening.

Review what you have heard to see if you have listened well. Practice listening. Become conscious of your listening skills.

The Importance of Listening

You listen to be helpful to yourself and to others.
You listen to obtain facts, to get the news, to hear the latest.
You listen to form an opinion, to reach a decision.
You listen to discover attitudes and feelings.
You listen to obtain feedback.
It is just good manners to listen attentively.

Five Requirements for Good Listening

Good listening requires restraint and constraint. You will have to take control of yourself and make yourself listen. It calls for having self-restraint all the way.

There must be a steady mental focus and singleness of purpose if your retention percentage is good. Retention depends upon attention.

Calmness and perseverance are a must. One should practice patience with self and with the speaker. Do not jump to conclusions or form quick attitudes and opinions.

Become involved in the dialogue: you, as the listener, and the other person as the speaker. If you listen well, the speaker will be better than expected. Your reaction is an action affecting him or her.

Seek for intelligent understanding. Keep your ears open. Plug up the holes in your mind. An open mind is good to let in the facts and sounds.

9
How to Study

Introduction

Have you ever said, "Oh me, I gotta study; I don't want to, and I don't have time"? Maybe you have uttered the first part of that statement without expressing a feeling or an excuse. I hope you have, and that you said it with commitment, joy, and anticipation. I haven't learned any way students can complete, their studies without studying. Studying appears to many students to be a barnacle hanging heavily around their necks throughout college days. But it isn't!

I hope I can dispel any negative feelings you may have regarding the privilege of studying.

Eight Reasons Why You Should Anticipate Studying

It is the best way to prepare for career success. Knowledge doesn't come automatically. Basic academic skills must be developed and honed.

Of course, you study to make the grade, so necessary in moving from one academic year to another. Very few, if any, can pass a course without studying. If that is true, something is wrong with the professor.

Studying is self-satisfying. There is joy in learning how to speak and write correctly. A thrill comes in learning new facts and new ideas.

Study quenches the basic human thirst for knowledge.

To develop your own efficiency, you must study. A pianist must practice. A singer must vocalize. Efficiency comes from repetition. Practice makes for perfection.

Opportunities abound, and you must prepare to take advantage of them. Opportunities have a way of vanishing if not seized.

Studying is good insurance against failure.

Your talents, mind, body, and soul are gifts from God, and you and I owe our best to Him in return.

How to Study More Effectively

Suggestions abound on how to improve study habits. None of them works unless you are willing to work at them. I have tried to group seven suggestions in a logical and concise manner, even using an alliterative method of listing for easier memorization.

Create Conditions Conducive to Study

Select and prepare a place of study. Let it become your regular study shrine. Be sure that the place is well ventilated, quiet, and comfortable. One cannot do well studying in the heart of a little O'Hare Airport. Excessive noises are a decided detriment to effective study. A stuffy area tends to cause drowsiness. Fresh air is invigorating.

Adequate lighting will prevent your eyes from becoming tired and will assist you greatly in understanding and comprehension. It is good if the light can fall over your left shoulder.

Try to maintain good eating habits. Stuffiness in the "tummy" also puts weight on the mind. Rich and heavy foods consume most of your body's energy for digestion. Equally hurtful is dependence upon stimulants such as cola drinks, coffee, tea, and so forth, because of the letdown aftereffects.

Most students tend to stay up too late at night, losing too much sleep. If you do, the next day your energy level will be low, and your spirit will sag. Get ample sleep.

Collect All Materials Needed for Study

Your textbooks should be handy. Much time can be lost in

careless placement of your textbooks. The assignment should be clear.

Have any needed reference materials at hand. Leaving your place of study to get something you have forgotten wastes time and breaks your concentration.

Have a good dictionary at arm's length. Do not gloss over any word, the meaning of which is fuzzy to you. Look it up. Fix it and some of its synonyms in your mind. It is helpful to have a thesaurus close by.

There should be adequate paper and pencils/pens. This might seem rather trite, but you can waste much time scrounging around hunting these. I think it is a smart policy to have a notebook for each class. Make notes. Underscore important facts and ideas—thus have a ruler.

Consume Allocated Time with Concentrated Effort

Schedule a time for study and allocate that time in light of the amount of study you need. Avoid being haphazard—a terrible foe of efficiency.

Start on time. Stay on time. Use your time wisely, and guard your time with conviction and fervor.

Tackle the hardest assignment first while your mind is fresh and alert.

Read carefully and go step by step with accuracy. Understand what you read.

Make copious notes—useful notes. The memory is enhanced as you write it down on paper.

Organize facts, figures, and ideas. This is pivotal. Notes taken, ideas gained, and figures accumulated are of little value if you cannot find them instantly.

Reread and review. You may need to reread only salient facts or first sentences of paragraphs, but take the time to have a memorable concept of what you have read. Spend time in reviewing.

When convenient, verbalize what you have studied with another student if this is not inconvenient. A fellow classmate is an appropriate person to involve in this activity.

Do whatever is necessary to keep your mind on track. Don't let it wander or fly out of the window and consort with pleasant memories. Stay at the helm. You are the captain. Prepare, organize, get with it, stay with it, and keep it fresh and available.

Control Your Study Habits, Schedules, and Techniques

These don't operate like perpetual motion. Approach your study time with considerable respect for the time and the purpose. There is nothing second rate about studying. Give it first-rate respect.

Look forward to the time you spend with your assignments. Keep negative thoughts out of your mind. Studying is not a chore. It is not a curse or a burden placed on students by the professor. Rather, it is an assignment that opens doors, provides new ideas, outlooks, and concepts. You are given the privilege of adding to your accumulation of knowledge. Consider it as placing more money in your savings account.

Strive arduously to improve. You will never arrive at Utopia. Increase your ability to concentrate, to apprehend, to organize, and to conserve. Become conscious of your progress as a runner would be of his desire to reduce the time it requires to run a mile.

It is possible to develop a workable, rhythmic stride of study. Avoid fighting desperately at the beginning and the ending. Have a smooth, consistent speed of preparation, and you will gain the most from your energy.

Push yourself to do the job as planned, even if you must call on your "second wind." Too many pauses during your allocated study time will disconnect your progress and short-circuit your efficiency.

Combat Your Worst Enemies

Do you have trouble following through and following up on your assignment preparations? Deal with this enemy immediately. Don't give in or else the habit will become stronger and harder to break.

If you feel tired, keep going after breathing deeply a few times and stretching while on tiptoes. You might walk over to the window and look into the distance for a minute, then return to your work area with the commitment to see it through.

Slow your pace a slight bit if you feel rushed. Fretting about the shortness of time only shortens your time. Keep your pace, your stride, operable. Unnecessary strain due to time constraints can work havoc. Haste makes waste. Make haste slowly.

Have you been guilty of procrastination? It is the thief of time, for the best time to do a thing is between yesterday and tomorrow. Fight the enemy of thinking you can do something better tomorrow rather than doing your best today. Read the handwriting on the wall before you get your back against the wall. If you put off something until tomorrow, how do you know you will do it tomorrow? You will probably be worse off tomorrow than today in breaking a bad habit.

Do you dislike studying? If so, do it until it feels good. I'm not trying to be a smart aleck. It is possible. I like many things today that I disliked yesterday, and the sweet taste has come out of keeping at the task.

The "call of the wild" lurks near by. Instincts clamor for expression. You will be beseiged by desires to drop your study and roam around. Look out, or you'll be ambushed by the killers of time.

Cope with Your Eccentricities

You have them: don't be deceived or led astray. Here are a few most of us succumb to:

"I can study better if I leave my radio on, so I'll not miss my favorite program." That's not so.

"I can do better even if the TV is on." Not true.

"I study better after 10:00 PM." Why?

"I love to lie down and study." Wooph! Look out, that lovely spirit of sleep will entice you into her fold.

"I like to sprawl in a chair with my feet higher than my head." That is really not a good way to force blood to your head. You are emphasizing the wrong end.

"Whenever necessary, I can always stay up all night." It should never be necessary unless a dire emergency has arisen. The drastic breaking of your normal routine is not very productive. You need sleep, and if first things come first, you can avoid the all-night marathon.

Evaluate Your Study Habits, Progress, and Efficiency

Think about your weaknesses. List them. Think about your strengths. Enumerate them. Now, plan how to overcome your weaknesses and, at the same time, maintain your strengths.

Elwood Chapman in his book, *College Survival,* includes a check list of study problems in which he mentions such matters as: feeling confused and depressed, sleepy, thinking about something totally unrelated and becoming fidgety and irritable when trying to read and concentrate.[1] Try to think of other problems arising when you attempt to study. Make your list. You will find it most profitable.

10
Making Full Use of Time

Introduction

I want you to notice that I did not title this chapter "How to Save Time." To me that would be a misunderstanding of time. You cannot save up time for a rainy day. You cannot provide a backlog of time. You can, however, do many things today in less time than years ago. You do not have to go to the well to draw water and then heat the water before you can bathe. Now all you have to do is turn on the water for the shower or tub. Instant coffee, instant oatmeal, and other items are on the market, making it possible for you to do things in less time, but that still means the most crucial thing for you and for me is to make full use of time. Quicker ways to do some things just give you more time to do more things better.

Benjamin Franklin observed, "The way to wealth is as plain as the market—waste neither time nor money, but make the best use of both."

I want to raise seven pertinent questions for your consideration and offer suggestions:

What is Time?

That's a mighty good question. Time is the staff of life. Time is money. Time is a measurement used in life, useful in developing a fuller life. Time is that something of which everyone at this present moment has an equal amount. Time goes on whether or not we go on. Time marches on. Time is divided into various segments for workable and livable purposes: the second, the minute, the hour, the day, the month, and the year. If you are now twenty and live to be eighty, you have 22,000 more days; every twenty-four hours is another day, but it will never return. Therefore, time is the most precious commodity you have. It comes one moment at a time, and that moment is gone before another one comes. You never have more than one moment at a time.

Time and tide wait for no one. Keep track of time lest time, as it goes on, leave you on the sidetrack.

How Much Time Do I Have?

You don't know, and I don't know. You have the present moment. Each day you live you have twenty-four hours consisting of morning, afternoon, and night. But we have all we need, and all we can get.

You would be very wise if you scheduled your time each day. Here is a very simple, yet functional, suggestion. Let us look at six days to the week, or 144 hours, leaving Sunday for the sabbath, for rest and worship. If you are taking sixteen credit hours per semester, that means:

16 hours in the classroom

32 hours in study (2 hours for each classroom hour. Schedule this!)

48 hours, classroom work and study

48 hours in sleep (8 hours per day)

48 hours for eating, grooming, and recreation (8 hours per day)

In other words, you have eight hours a day for classroom and study, eight hours a day for sleep, and eight hours a day for other things. If you treat time lightly, you will never have enough. If you "fill the unforgiving minute with sixty seconds worth of distance run," you will always have enough.

What Is Time Worth?

Who knows? It is not free or valueless. Time is very valuable. To waste time is the same as throwing money into a deep well. It produces nothing. A lost pearl may be found, but lost time never, yet the time may be more valuable than the pearl.

Ponder This for a Few Seconds

It has been said that life with a college education is worth half-a-million dollars more than life without a college education.

Thirty weeks will comprise two semesters. Seven days a week, twenty-four hours a day, equals 168 hours per week, or 5,040 hours per year.

Four years of college education at thirty weeks per year equals 20,160 hours, or 5,040 hours per year.

This, divided into half-a-million dollars makes each hour worth $24.80. That surely is much more than minimum wage. Are you rich enough to afford the loss of many hours? I doubt if you are, but extra application can even make the hours worth far more later on down the road.

I think you can see that time is not free, and it costs tremendously to waste or kill it.

What Are Some Dangerous Time Wasters?

They seem to swarm around us daily. Indecision is one. It is like marking time or racing a motor in neutral.

Laziness is another. Build a fire under laziness, and burn out the indolence and slothfulness. Use your energy else it will clog your channels of achievement.

Lack of a plan is one. Going around in circles trying to find the right direction is like a ship without a rudder. It is folly of follies to mount an iron steed and ride off madly in every direction. You should plan carefully each day. Know where you are going.

Dealing in nonessentials or secondary matters is a time waster. Little is accomplished while important things go unattended.

Too much time spent at the snack bar drinking soft drinks or coffee can put unnecessary pressure on your time schedule.

Puttering around the edges, warming your feet in the edge of the pool, is a killer of time. Plunge in. Go to the heart of things.

Putting off until tomorrow what should be done today is a waste of time, for it takes time from both days, and what is put off may never be done.

Excuse making and attempting to justify our inaction waste a lot of time.

Stay alert! Slay the dragons of wastefulness.

How Can I Make Effective Use of My Time?

Realize the value of time and work out a schedule of all daily activities from awakening in the morning until sleep comes in the evening. Of course, that schedule may be interrupted, but if you have eight hours a day for miscellaneous activities, you will be able to handle interruptions. However, keep your work schedule and your sleep schedule inviolate.

Even with a good schedule, you will need to set definite priorities at a definite time. Some things must come first, others second, and the priorities will change from time to time, which means you need to be able to adjust, and adjustments can be time-savers, not time-wasters.

Much has been spoken about energy cycles. Study your energy cycles and schedule loads accordingly.

Do some things which everyone else has to do when everyone else isn't doing them. Everyone can't eat in the cafeteria at the same time. There are bound to be peak loads which you will want to avoid. Everyone can't play tennis at the same time. Do these things when the amount of time standing in line is practically nil.

You may be able to group certain tasks and thereby decrease the amount of time in doing them singly by doing them conjunctively.

You will have to factor in the habits and personalities of people: roommate, friends, and so forth, in order to budget your time and stay on schedule.

You will need to learn how to handle interruptions. They are sure to arise. Be understanding but be decisive.

Remember, time is precious, and each hour is valuable. Someone once mused, "Be clock-eyed to avoid doing cockeyed things."

Is It Possible to Make Time Deposits?

This may seem like a superfulous question since you cannot store up time, but stay with me a minute or so more. I have a few suggestions. First, extra-curricular reading stores up information and knowledge which down the road will save time and simplify matters. Second, have a personal idea file. Let it become a future storehouse where you can retrieve information. Don't let the cupboard become bare. Third, keep a notebook or notepad handy. (Pardon a personal reference, but I keep one at my bedside.) Additionally, carry one in your purse or pocket to jot down salient information. Fourth, learn how to avoid waiting.

Take Time to Check How You Are Handling Time

Answer the following questions* and evaluate yourself. If your score is not acceptable, what do you intend to do about it?

Time management is important. Learn the art.

Check your skills to determine if you use the following timesaving techniques.

1. I set a deadline for every goal.   1 2 3 4 5
2. I don't trust my memory. I carry a pad and jot things down.   1 2 3 4 5
3. I make sure each job is done the most economical way.   1 2 3 4 5
4. I work to improve my reading skills. I phrase read and skim efficiently. 1 2 3 4 5
5. I have devised a foolproof reminder system.   1 2 3 4 5
6. I consolidate activities—phone calls, correspondence, etc.   1 2 3 4 5
7. Meetings are expensive and time consum-

ing. I give advance notice of subject matter, keep on target, don't let it bog down.   1 2 3 4 5

8. I avoid gabfests.   1 2 3 4 5

9. I tackle my most demanding tasks in my most productive hours.   1 2 3 4 5

10. Once a decision is made—if there's no longer anything I can do about it—my best bet is to forget it and go on to the next project.   1 2 3 4 5

11. Neatness counts. The philosophy of "a place for everything and everything in its place" is a smart one to live by.   1 2 3 4 5

12. I try to spend some time alone each day. (Your best ideas will strike when pondering problems by yourself.)   1 2 3 4 5

13. I coordinate activities for an even flow of the work.   1 2 3 4 5

14. I have learned to say "no" when I should say "no." I don't saddle myself with unessential tasks just to be obliging.   1 2 3 4 5

15. I anticipate my needs and the needs of others. I'm not a last-minute panic-button pusher.   1 2 3 4 5

16. I try to complete each task I tackle without having to come back a second time.   1 2 3 4 5

17. If a task is difficult or unpleasant, I try to dispose of it as quickly as possible.   1 2 3 4 5

18. I stay alert to mechanized short cuts.   1 2 3 4 5

19. I get off to an early start. I organize, review or revise priorities at the beginning of each day.   1 2 3 4 5

20. I put a high price tag on my minutes and hours. I get real achievement or real enjoyment out of every waking hour.   1 2 3 4 5

Score   _____ [1]

11
How to Take Tests

Introduction

You will notice I did not say *examinations.* Somehow I feel the word *test* is better. Examination carries the idea of the physician and the patient, rather than the professor and the student. If we stay in the context of examination, the idea might emerge that in education final examinations are *final,* terminal, like saying, "You have incurable cancer." But, since I have chosen to use the word *test,* it is not a miracle word for the lethargic, the slothful, and the unprepared. Knowledge for tests does not come the night before while one is getting a good night's sleep.

Why Do You Have to Take Tests?

Couldn't tests be eliminated? Is very much accomplished cramming for a test and then taking it with anxiety and fear?

Tests provide the climate for comprehensive review of previous work. It is a time to go back and look at the ground that has been covered. An excellent review of work done previously is a helpful way to see it as a unit, and not as scattered intellectual bricks. The parts can be put together into a whole.

Tests are useful means of evaluating the work of the student especially through grades. Too much emphasis can be given to test scores, but proper evaluation is needed.

Tests help both student and professor to stress and understand what is most vital. Tests are not given to trap *students* or to fail some and pass others. There is no joy or pride on the teacher's part in this. Taking a test is like playing a conference game on Saturday in contrast to all of the scrimmages during the week. It is a test of your remembrance of the important workable things you have learned.

To some students tests are periods of catch up. To follow this as a normal procedure is bad; however, this reason is a plus for students who have missed much due to emergencies, illness, and the like.

Tests stimulate and motivate for learning. Other reasons are there, and I am sure you could add several.

What Are the Various Kinds of Tests?

"Essay" tests are test questions so stated as to evoke thought as well as fact. Most of the questions rarely have a single correct answer. Answers to this type are usually written narratively, in an essay form, which allow for relationships, comparisons, and differences.

"True/false" tests, frequently given, basically test your ability to read critically. In taking this type of test you should look for the key words *always, never, all, greatest, or without reservation.* Recently, I heard Dr. Norman Shumate of the United States Army tell of sitting in on one of the army classes during a test. He noticed a soldier on the back row flipping a coin. Overcome with curiosity he went to the back of the classroom and inquired of the soldier why he was flipping a coin. The soldier replied, "Heads, it's true; tails, it's false. I'm getting my answers."

Later during the test he saw the same soldier resume the coin flipping, after he knew the soldier had finished answering all of the questions. "Soldier, what are you doing now?"

"Oh, Sir, I am checking my answers."

Personally, I don't care for a true/false test in most cases. Can you think of my reasons?

There are "multiple-choice" tests which are exactly what the word means: multiple choice. You are given several stated answers, only one of which is correct, and you are to choose which one of the answers is correct.

Some professors like to give an "open book" test. This occurs when you are allowed to use your textbook. A problem or question is raised, and you search for the answer. In this case, your professor is interested in knowing if you understand how to use information, tables, or equations.

Some of the Hindrances You May Face in Taking Tests

I am going to mention only four: fear, frustration, fatigue, and fidgetiness.

I hope you aren't fearful of tests. Fear will produce over anxiety, nervousness, and tension. Your fear could be enhanced and become more real if you have goofed off and come to the testing time unprepared. Don't get rattled. I had a friend who, while taking his doctoral examination in religion, was asked, "Who was the father of the sons of Zebedee?"

"I don't know," he replied. He was rattled. The answer was obvious.

Frustration may overcome you especially if you have failed to regulate your time and realize too late you do not have enough time to review adequately. You may have overslept the morning of the test and had to rush at the last minute to arrive there on time. You may have had an extra-heavy schedule for several days before and feel terribly frustrated with the mountain of work you have attempted. Pace yourself with confidence and fully use every moment.

Fatigue is a common enemy at test time. Staying up all night before an examination is unwise. Go to bed on time and get up on time. Don't drag yourself to the test as a condemned victim. Dress for the important occasion and make it a time of celebration. A tired mind, a tired body, and a heavy load are very incompatible with good work.

Fidgetiness is a disease that seems to come with tests. I have seen otherwise calm students come to test time in an awkward state of confusion. They can't seem to find the right seat. They don't seem to be comfortable. They are without adequate writing materials and paper. And most of all, they just can't seem to settle down and get with it.

How to Take Tests More Effectively

Maybe I should say, "There are tricks to all trades," but I don't feel that is quite apropos here.

Review carefully, fully, comprehensively, and orderly the work you are to be tested on. Try to recall that which the professor has emphasized. Review previous tests if they are available. Study your notes, the contents of the textbook, and any outside reading you have been assigned. Start this review earlier than the night before the test. Give yourself ample time to digest your review rather than just "crammin'."

Go to the testing place on time and relaxed. Don't panic, don't rush. Be ready, and go with your quiver full of arrows. Have a positive mental attitude about your upcoming experience. You are not about to become a martyr. You are not about to be offered as a sacrifice. It is your chance to perform, your chance to give back what you have received.

Read all the questions very carefully. This is especially important on essay tests. You need to read each question very carefully on true/false and multiple-choice tests.

Once a professor handed out test questions to his students with the admonition, "Now, please read all the questions carefully before you start writing." No one heeded the professor, for the tenth question read, "If you have read each of the previous questions very carefully, you will not need to take this test. Just hand in a blank paper with your name on it." No one followed the professor's advice.

Be sure you understand each question, and if not, ask for clarification.

Plan an organized procedure to answer the questions. Take the easiest question first. Next, take the one with the most points. Be sure you have saved enough time for the hardest questions.

Concentrate; avoid distractions. If someone finishes by the time you are only about half through, do not let that bother you. There are no Brownie points given to the one who finishes first.

If a question asks for theories and does not mention the number of theories, do not write there are five and then find yourself able to give only three. You have automatically admitted that you do not know two of the theories. Just state there are several and list the ones you know.

Attempt to answer each question. A freshman goofed off before Judgment Day came. Question number four asked, "Please give the quotation you have memorized from Robert Browning." The freshman could not recall the specific quotation, but he did recall an instruction given during orientation to write something, so he penned, "The roast was in the oven, browning." I think I would have given him some points for creativity and ingenuity.

Write logically, clearly, neatly, and correctly. It is very hard for a professor to give points when a question is answered in a manner reminiscent of a garbage heap that must be dug through in order to find an answer. Disconnected thoughts, dangling in thin blue air, indicate a bit of confusion.

Take all tests with integrity. Do not sell your honor down the river just to make a passing grade or a better grade. Dean Madison Sarratt, formerly of Vanderbilt University, would say to his class in trigonometry, "Today I am going to give you two examinations: one in trigonometry and one in honesty. I hope you pass both of them. If you fail one, let it be trigonometry."

Cheating is rather prevalent these days. Students have become clever and adept at cheating. May I urge you to refrain from weakening your character qualities by cheating. Do you want a doctor who cheats while operating on you?

Save enough time to review your answers. This is very vital. In haste, you may have written something in error. Reviewing your answers is like polishing your shoes or combing your hair. Hand in your answers to the professor with a fairly true indication of your best.

Have a good time. Stand up to the test.

12
How to Improve Your Grades

Introduction

I'm going to hit you with two questions: Do your grades need improving? If your grades do improve, is that of significance? If your answer to the first is yes, then the general assumption is that the answer to the second would be yes. But never forget, the second is not automatically yes especially as relates to success later in life.

Grades are not everything, but they do say something. Grades don't tell the whole story. Grades just for grades' sake are of little value. Are you a member of the recent grade mania? Go for grades, but go for life principles.

Take a Look at the Grading System

As you sought admission to college you took either the ACT (American College Test) or the SAT (Scholastic Aptitude Test). If you scored between 25 and 30, you made a good score on the ACT with 36 being a perfect score. The test was comprised of four divisions: science, mathematics, English, and social studies. If you scored between 1100 and 1375 on the SAT, you did well. If your score fell in either of the ranges given above, you have a good chance of doing well in college but with no assurance of good college grades or success in life.

Most educational institutions use the following grading system:

A — 95-100
B — 87- 94

C   —   77- 86
D   —   70- 76   (lowest passing grade)
F   —   below 70

It is generally assumed that the higher your scores are by either the ACT or SAT method, the higher your college grades will be. *But, wait!*

What is your IQ (Intelligence Quotient) score? There is definitely a correlation between one's IQ and ACT or SAT scores and grades. But, wait!

What are your MQ (Motivation Quotient) and DQ (Determination Quotient) scores? You don't know? That's right, for there have not been any tests devised that can measure those quotients accurately. The real test is inside you. Motivation and determination can take an average scorer and work wonders. Accumulated facts and vast knowledge must be coupled with imagination, motivation, and determination.

What Are the Ingredients of a Grade?

Regular attendance in class is a component of a good grade. A student needs to hear the professor's lectures and keep up with all of the work to score well.

Daily assignments must be handled well.

Tests are given frequently. You should score well on all pop tests, mid-semester tests, and final tests.

Quality work on term papers or outside assignments is important.

Your spirit and attitude are vitally necessary if you are to test well.

Why are Grades Important?

Grades provide a type of measurement or indication of growth, mastery of the subject, and general knowledge acquired. Grades should indicate progress.

Grades indicate the quality of success you have made in covering the material and purpose of a course of study. Grades do not indicate what you can do but rather what you have done.

Grades are considered in granting scholarships, in gaining admission to graduate schools, and in acquiring jobs. Other factors are also considered such as leadership qualities, ability to make value judgments, industry, and integrity.

If good grades do indicate good students, then the teacher is pleased and, in most cases, puts out more for student consumption.

A Few "Don'ts" in Your Quest for Improved Grades

1. Don't try to "apple polish" your instructor. It'll be somewhat like the blood of Duncan on Lady Macbeth's hand: it won't rub off, and it will be self-incriminating. I don't know many, if any, instructors, teachers, or professors who give grades because of such behavior.

2. Don't go just for the grade. You may get it, but you have gotten an empty basket with no fruit.

3. Don't let the tension of grade-making drive you into unreasonable activities.

4. Don't cheat in order to make grades. In fact, don't cheat. It's tempting at times if you need a certain grade. Don't be a traitor to your own best self.

Thirty Ways to Improve Your Grades

Harry Shaw wrote in 1976 a book entitled: *Thirty Ways to Improve Your Grades,* and it is worth every bit of the purchase price.[1]

With the permission of the publishers, I am listing those thirty ways, adding only my brief comment under each.

1. *Uncover your attitudes.*
   Have a positive attitude toward your professors, your books, your fellow students and alma mater. You are effective by your attitude.
2. *Change some of your work habits.*

Habits that are allowed to grow become very difficult to break. Establish good study habits and respect those habits.

3. *Take care of your body and brain.*

You have only one body, only one brain. Learn their potential and protect them with tender, loving care.

4. *Find your best place and time for study.*

Get yourself a little shrine of study. Keep it conducive to study and keep sacred the time allocated for study.

5. *Work within a time budget.*

Schedule your time to meet the demands and obligations, and don't waste time.

6. *Try to think logically and clearly.*

Think clearly, without confusion. Put your reason into operation. Think before acting.

7. *Understand what you read.*

The question is not, Did you read? but, What did you read? Read with an undivided mind.

8. *Get rid of bad reading habits.*

(Refer to chapter 7: *"How to Increase Reading Skills."*)

9. *Train your memory to commit itself.*

Put your memory to the test. Listen well. Properly stack what you garner in your mind.

10. *Learn to listen while listening to learn.*

(Refer to chapter 8: *"How to Listen."*)

11. *Put into your own words what you read and hear.*

Let what you read and hear become a part of you, with your own distinctive flavor and expression.

12. *Take notes in precise form.*

Take notes, but not too many. Take sensible notes, and may your notes make sense when later you refer to them.

13. *View and then review.*

Take a good look at the general and the specific; then be sure you have not substituted the specific for the general and vice versa.

14. *Learn to talk with people.*

Discuss things with others. Get a second opinion.

15. *Learn to talk to people.*

Be precise. Be pleasant. May your words be well articulated. Be informative.

16. *Say it right.*

Really, there should be no other way. Hit the nail on the head.

17. *Make friends with your dictionary.*

By all means, do this. Your dictionary has a world of knowledge in it, more than just the meanings of words. Keep it handy.

18. *Increase your vocabulary.*

This will make it possible for you to say it better, make it stick, and expand its meaning.

19. *Say exactly what you mean.*

Don't beat around the bush. Don't be verbose. Don't gild the lily. Say it!

20. *Don't be a rubber stamp.*

It's terribly monotonous, drab, and boring to be a rubber stamp. Stretch your own imagination and creative powers.

21. *Get rid of dead wood.*

Have a mental housecleaning. Build a big bonfire. Throw away the nonessentials.

22. *Take seven steps to better sentences.*

Let all sentences be written properly, with unity, correct spelling, and punctuation. All sentences should be spoken with unity, brevity, and clearness.

23. *Spell it right.*

Why not? It is much easier, clearer, and absolutely important.

24. *Punctuate it right.*

If you don't look out, faulty punctuation will say something you do not desire said.

25. *Divide and conquer.*

Prepare some kind of outline for each question. The outline should be logical, progressive, and comprehensive.

26. *Discover your library.*

Go into your storehouse and bring out relevant, additional
   information. Eat more than a cheese-and-crackers diet.

27. *Take three steps to better papers and reports.*

Here are three: *research adequately, write clearly, logically,
   and accurately,* and then *rewrite for refinement.*

28. *Write legibly.*

Your writing is in vain if it has to be deciphered or is illegible.

29. *Revise and proofread everything you write.*

What more could be said?

30. *Improve your test-taking methods*

Well, that is what the previous twenty-nine ways are all
   about. Get with it.

Grades are important, but mesh your efforts to make good
grades with motivation, determination, creativity, and enthusiasm. Hitch these horses to your grade wagon.

May your capability in making better grades be a part of your
intellectual development and not merely an end in itself. May the
making of good grades suggest that you can also make a good life
by putting together the proper components. It is not a matter of
luck.

13
Using the Library

Introduction

"How many volumes do you have in your library?" inquired a sophisticated freshman of the dean.

"Oh," replied the dean, "75,000."

"Just 75,000," said the young man.

"Yes sir, but when you have finished those 75,000, we will have a few more."

It is still true that a book is a new book until you have read it. A library is:

A depository of books,
   ranging from a few hundred to millions of volumes;
A center of information,
A house of knowledge.

Knowledge is twofold.

Since you can't know everything, the next best thing is knowing where to find it. Once you have gained the skill of how to use a library, any resource in it is available to you, and a skill in obtaining and using such information is one mark of an educated person.

A Library Consists of More than Books

Foremost, a library is books in rows or stacks. There are two kinds of stacks: open stacks and closed stacks. Students are free to go among open stacks to secure the books they need. In some cases this saves time, but if you are given to scanning, it can waste time. In using the closed stacks, secure the call number of the book you want from the card files and ask for assistance at the desk. A staff member will get the book or books for you. There is a circulation desk where all books are checked out and returned on or before the date due.

Most professors ask librarians to place certain books on reserve, a shelf or designated place where they are easily available while the course is in session. Usually any book on reserve cannot be checked out overnight. Different libraries have different rules for reserve.

The *reference section* of the library is very useful. Become acquainted with this area, since it contains books of statistical information and facts in almost any discipline.

A *microform area* of microfilm and microfiche contains reels of film, flat fiche, and equipment to help you read and print hard copies of text material.

Newspapers, journals, and *periodicals* are located in a special section and can be found easily. They contain timely articles on specialized subjects. Some periodical index is always available. The one most used is *The Readers' Guide to Periodical Literature,* indexed by author, title, and subject.

Reading rooms are provided for the convenience of users. Rooms are of two types: one, for anyone to use; and a section for certain individuals, usually outfitted with carrels for graduate students or a specially designated group.

The *card file,* normally referred to as the card catalog (or an automated catalog if the library is very modern), is the heart of any library and is most important. You should become well acquainted with it. There are two classification schedules currently in use in most libraries, the Library of Congress Classification System and the Dewey Decimal Classification System. The Library of Congress system is gaining favor with academic libraries and automated systems although either serves adequately. All books are cataloged by author, title and subject with a card for each. Here are some examples.[1]

ATHLETES—RELIGIOUS LIFE.

BV
4596   King, LeRoy, ed.
.A8   Courage to conquer; America's
K56   athletes speak their faith / edited by
1966

       Co., c1966
          127 p. 21 cm.

       1. Athletes—Religious life.   I.
Title

Additional Helps in the Use of the Library

Ask a librarian if there are annotated bibliographies available for various disciplines. If so, secure one covering the academic area of your concern. Most librarians are willing to help users find any resource they need.

Learn the reference books in your academic discipline. As an example, if you are interested in literature, find the Biography of Contemporary Authors (mostly authors of the twentieth century). This work will be helpful to you. Do the same for other disciplines.

For a synopsis of a book, quotation, poem or some aspect of religion, and so forth, see Magill's reference books under appropriate titles. Example: *Magill's Quotation in Context; Magill's Literary Annual.*

If you are working on a term paper turn to Chapter 15 and review the section on "Search Strategy for a Research Paper."

Remember that the card catalog is a dictionary catalog . . . meaning that the cards (author, title, subject) are arranged in one

TNSB-S 21 DEC 88   712126   TNEEdc   66-21798

Courage to conquer

BV
4596   King, LeRoy, ed.
.A8   Courage to conquer; America's
K56   athletes speak their faith / edited by
1966   Leroy King. Westwood, N.J.: F. H. Revell
          Co., c1966
               127 p. 21 cm.

               1. Athletes—Religious life.   I.
          Title

TNSB-S 21 DEC 88   712126   TNEEdc   66-21798

BV
4596   King, LeRoy, ed.
.A8   Courage to conquer; America's
K56   athletes speak their faith / edited by
1966   Leroy King. Westwood, N.J.: F. H. Revell
          Co., c1966
               127 p. 21 cm.

               1. Athletes—Religious life.   I.
          Title

TNSB-S 21 DEC 88   712126   TNEEsl   66-21798

LIBRARY OF CONGRESS CLASSIFICATION
SCHEDULES

Classes A to Z:

A	General works: Polygraphy.
B	Philosophy and Religion:
	Part I, B–BJ: Philosophy.
	Part II, BL–BX: Religion.
C	History: Auxiliary Sciences.
D	History: General and Old World.
E–F	History: America.
G	Geography, Anthropology, Folklore, etc.
H	Social Sciences.
J	Political Science.
K	Law.
	KF: Law of the United States.
L	Education.
M	Music.
N	Fine Arts.
P	Philology and Literature:
	P-PA: Philology. Classical Philology and Literature.
	PA Supplement: Byzantine and Modern Greek Literature. Medieval and Modern Latin Literature.
	PB-PH: Modern European Languages.
	PG: Russian Literature.
	PJ-PM: Languages and Literatures of Asia, Africa, Oceania, America; Mixed Languages; Artificial Languages.
	P-PM Supplement: Index to Languages and Dialects.
	PN, PR, PS, PZ: Literature—General, English, American. Fiction and Juvenile Literature.
	PQ, Part 1: French Literature.
	PQ, Part 2: Italian, Spanish, Portuguese Literatures.
	PT, Part 1: German Literature.
	PT, Part 2: Dutch and Scandinavian Literatures.
Q	Science.
R	Medicine.
S	Agriculture, etc.
T	Technology.
U	Military Science.
V	Naval Science.
Z	Bibliography and Library Science.[2]

DEWEY DECIMAL CLASSIFICATION SYSTEM

Here are the ten major divisions, and examples of some of their subdivisions:[3]

000—General Works:
   028 How to Read a Book
   028.5 Good Books for Children
100—Philosophy:
   130 Psychology
   136.7 Emotional Problems of Adolescence
200—Religion:
   220 Bible
   226 New Testament
   226.8 Parables of Jesus
300—Social Sciences:
   321 Labor Movement
   331.1 Collective Bargaining
400—Grammar Languages:
   420 English Language
   423.1 Dictionary of English Idioms
500—Science:
   550 Earth Sciences
   551.1 Weather
600—Useful Arts:
   621 Mechanical Engineering
   621.2 Hydraulic Machinery
700—Fine Arts:
   770 Photography
   778.1 Photographic Enlarging
800—Literature:
   822 English Plays
   822.3 Shakespeare
900—History, Travel, Biography:
   970 North American history
   970.1 North American Indians
   910 Travel
   914 European Travel
   914.1 Travel in Scotland
   920 Collective Biography

alphabetical sequence and you may look for books in three ways: by author, subject, and title. The last name of the author is given first and this author's card is referred to as the MAIN ENTRY CARD. Books are listed by titles but ignore *a, an,* or *the* at the beginning of the title. All books containing information on specific subjects are listed in the card catalog under words or phrases describing those subjects.

Common Mistakes Made by Students in the Use of the Library

Timidity, which causes the student to refrain from asking for help. *If you aren't sure, ask, ASK.*

The *scanning* of open stacks with the hope of finding something relating to what you are looking for. This is a misuse of time.

Lack of patience in your search. Most libraries contain more resources than you can use. Don't stop with one book or one article for you may have missed the best.

Failure to become acquainted with the resources of the library and how they are organized. You should know the library as well as you know the contents and function of your dormitory or gymnasium.

Lastly, and the most pathetic, is being obsessed with the feeling of *"Why go to the library?* Why not stay with the textbook?" Doing this is like eating a one-course meal when six more courses are available to you. Beat a path to the library. Use it.

What an Opportunity!

Library Automation

During the past decade academic libraries have moved steadily towards automation. Computerized catalogs, which contain all the information of conventional card catalogs, have more searching capabilities, and are becoming commonplace. In addition, a number of libraries offer on-line searching of external databases via telephone lines to resources located in far away cities. Once connected to the host computer, the user can choose among options from copying the bibliographic citation from the screen to receiving the full text of a periodical article later by mail. A third wave of technology currently sweeping the library world is CD-ROM (compact disk-read only memory), which has the capability of storing the content of hundreds of books or thousands of periodical articles on a single compact disk. (It takes approximately three thousand floppy disks to store the data of one CD-ROM disk.)

To illustrate the dramatic impact of computers on student use of the library, let us follow Mary Smith as she works on a research paper. Mary has already selected a research topic which her professor has approved. She understands that the paper should include material from periodicals as well as books. She decides to search book material before she undertakes the periodical search.

To locate appropriate books, Mary uses one of several computer terminals located throughout the library. Although she has no prior experience with computers, she is undaunted, having seen a brief demonstration of the library's computer system in an orientation session. Futhermore, the instructor insisted that the library computer is "user friendly." Following the simple instructions posted at the terminal, Mary calls up a menu screen, which provides basic choices. For example, she can search for books by author, title, subject, or even a single key word.

As she proceeds with her search, Mary soon realizes how much more flexible and encompassing the computer catalog is compared to the library's old card catalog. She discovers she can even search a specific segment of the collection (such as art), or a particular resource format (such as filmstrips). She is especially pleased that the system also allows Boolean searching (combining two or more terms) to narrow her topic more precisely—for example combining the terms *"exercise"* and *"heart"* to retrieve books which deal with the effect of exercise on cardiovascular development. Receiving frequent screen prompts which guide her search, Mary soon locates several books on her topic. For each record the terminal has supplied the book's call number and its availability status.

After completing the book search, Mary is ready to begin a search for periodical articles. Although she has the option of doing a search of manual indexes, such as the *Reader's Guide to Periodical Literature* or the *General Science Index,* Mary asks the reference librarian to perform a computerized search. Since such a search entails long-distance telephone charges and other fees levied by the data base vendor, Mary expects to pay for this search. The librarian explains that for an additional fee, the bibliographic citations can be printed on-line while Mary waits. Mary, however, opts to have the citations printed off-line and sent to the library within a few days.

Last of all, Mary needs some numerical data to help illuminate her topic. Instead of searching through numerous statistical sources, she turns to the library's CD-ROM microcomputer into which she loads a statistical data disk. In a few minutes after inputting selected key words from her research topic, she sees on the screen a compilation of figures which will enhance her paper. In another moment she has in hand a paper copy of the data produced by the printer connected to the CD-ROM.

As Mary leaves the library she stops at the circulation desk to check out the books she has located. She hands her bar-coded ID card to the desk attendant who zips a light-wand across it. Mary's name displays on the computer screen as the attendant zips the light wand across the bar code on each of the books. Within seconds Mary is on her way, without having had to fill out a single card or sign her name. Her search for materials was quick, productive, and thorough. She saved additional time in the borrowing process—all of which she attributes to the library's integrated computer system. She is impressed.[4]

14
How to Take Notes

Introduction

You are probably going to react immediately with: "Why devote a chapter on how to take notes? I know how. Just take them—that's all."

But I am both sad and glad to say, "That's not all." I am sad to make it sound so difficult, but I'm glad to be able to offer you some helpful suggestions.

There is a legend that a man was walking in the desert and heard a voice saying to him, "Pick up some stones and put them in your pocket. Tomorrow you will be both sad and glad that you did this." The man obeyed. The next day he reached into his pocket to remove the stones, and to his amazement the stones had turned to rubies, diamonds, and emeralds. He was elated that he had taken some stones but sad that he had not taken more. So it is with education and note taking.

Note-taking is an art
    and, therefore, very important and valuable.
Note-taking can be most helpful;
    therefore, the notes must be available.
Note-taking is a secondary aid
    and must not replace intense listening.
Note-taking is a good assurance policy,
    so don't let it lapse.

Why Take Notes?

I see only three major aspects of note-taking: why take notes, how to take notes, and, if you take notes, use your notes.

Here are six basic reasons why you should take classroom notes or notes on a book you have read or information you may have gathered outside the classroom or off campus:

Note-taking is a must for formal educational survival. It may be possible for a student to pass a course without taking notes, especially in math or some science, but that would be an exception, not the rule. Those who may be prone to complain about note-taking early in a course will complain much more at the end of the course if they have taken no notes.

Note-taking helps one to understand the lecture and classroom discussion. It gets the listener and the note taker involved. When you are taking notes, you cannot be passive: you are involved. As you put the main ideas on paper, it helps to make the lecture much clearer.

Notes are a great asset for review of course content and for preparation for tests and final examinations. Your notes should provide for you both the heart and salient facts of the course. You will have available for review notes you have taken during the class periods and notes for your own preparation. If you have taken your notes carefully and logically, then you are reviewing "the meat of the coconut."

Education is costly. A father was heard to remark, "Sure, reading and writing will provide an education for my son. He does the reading, and I do the writing—of checks." Someone does have to pay the high costs of education. It doesn't make sense to me that some students do their best not to get full value received for money spent. The taking of good notes provides a much better return on your investment.

Notes taken and preserved can be of great help later in life.

Pardon this personal reference, but I still refer to notes I made during my educational days. I have been back to that watering trough many times.

Form the habit of taking good notes now. It will be useful to you later on, and the habit of note-taking will continue and therefore enhance the value of your present learning how to do it well.

How to Take Notes

One early caution: be sure that words don't go into your ears and out of your finger tips. That type of note-taking is formal only and of little value. In fact, it is of negative value because time was diverted from listening while notes were being scribbled.

Get yourself a notebook, preferably loose-leaf, for each course you are taking. This will keep you from having one page of notes from your English class, the next page of notes from your French class, and the third page from your social-studies class. This kind of note-taking may bring confusion and distraction. Pay homage and respect to your notebooks. It will become to you what the black bag is to the physician, what a tool kit is to the carpenter, and what the music score is to the pianist. Be proud of your notebook, both inside and outside. Avoid taking notes in a small notebook. It will discourage you from taking sufficient notes.

Listen before your write. Think about what you are going to put into your notes before you start writing so you can select the important points stressed by the professor. You won't be able to put down everything your professor says, and you won't need to put down everything your professor says. I know from experience. I have been both student and professor. Careful listening is so priceless. If something strikes you as important, or if the professor says it is important, think before you put anything on paper in order to record that important information properly.

Organize, outline, and write correctly and legibly. There are several ways to write notes:

Type A: Type B: Type C:

_____	_____:	1. _____
_____	_____	_____ .
_____ .	_____ .	_a._ _____
	_____ .	2. _____
		_____ .

The student who writes like the outline of *Type A,* one sentence after another, has notes that are difficult to read and less useful. *Type B* is in topical form and could also be in question form. Good ways. *Type C* is in outline form, a great procedure if you do not run ahead of the lecturer and get your outline out of sequence.

Outline and underline your notes if time permits and you have good judgment about what to underline. The circling of a number or statistic is also helpful.

As a time-saver use symbols, abbreviations, or even shorthand if you are always able to decipher such. Unless you are proficient in shorthand, it may be cold later on. Writing in longhand has the same tendency if your writing is done too hastily or carelessly.

If time permits, at the end of the course, organize the notes taken by doing some sort of general outline or table of contents.

Use Your Notes

Take good care of your notes and use them. There is value in taking notes; take notes systematically and carefully and use them regularly and continuously.

PS: This suggestion may be of some help to you (another personal reference). I keep a notebook and pencil in a container hanging on the side of my bed. I use it frequently because I am prone to have both early morning and late-at-night thoughts which, in the rush of the day or the fatigue of the evening, might vanish quickly. I try to lasso them and corral them into my notebook.

15
How to Write a Research Paper

Introduction

Writing a research paper can actually be fun and exciting because it will involve: ingenuity and creativity in the selection of a topic, patience as you discover amazing ideas, and joy which comes from putting it all together into a finished product.

In his *Essay on Criticism,* Alexander Pope wrote:

> True ease in writing comes from art, not chance,
> As those move easiest who have learn'd to dance.

It is not possible to do a research paper at the last minute. You cannot find one in a "put-it-together" kit. The best research paper, from your standpoint, is one you birth, feed, nurture, and support.

Many articles, pamphlets, and books have been written on how to do a research paper, and I am not so conceited as to think I can add any brilliance to what has already been done. I have followed none of the sources in particular but mine, which comes from reading, experience, and practice. My sole purpose here is to give you clear, logical steps to take in writing a good research paper.

On the pages which follow I have presented: (1) Form of Research Paper and (2) Procedure in Writing Research Papers. If you will study these first before attempting to do anything on your paper, I think you will be able to proceed more orderly and logically. Please don't commit the unpardonable sin of starting to write before you have done the preliminary work of researching, outlining, and organizing.

Form of Research Paper

I. Title page

This should include the title of the paper, why the paper is written: In fulfillment of _____ Class, professor's name, college, your name, and date.

II. Outline of paper

This should include introduction, theme, statement of main points of thesis in outline form, author's conclusion, and summary.

III. Body of paper

Here the author will want to develop each point of the theme with support information in accordance with the outline.

IV. Appendixes

Included in the appendixes will be exhibits, charts, graphs, tables, etc.

V. Bibliography

An alphabetical listing by author of books or periodicals consulted.

This cannot be done at the beginning but must take shape as the result of fully developing each step—from the first to the last—of the procedure as given on the next page.

Each section should follow the previous one, as listed.

Procedure in Writing Research Papers

I.   Select a topic.

II.   Do a preliminary investigation and reading of available material in order to state in one sentence the theme of your paper.

III.   Research the topic adequately.

IV.   Organize the material you have on your notes which you have garnered from your researching the topic.

V.   Outline your material.

VI.   Write a rough first draft with accurate footnotes.

VII.   Revise critically—as to logic, development, punctuation, etc.—for the final draft.

VIII.   Rewrite the final draft with appendixes and bibliography.

Each of these points will be discussed in the same sequence on the following pages.

Procedures in Writing Research Papers

Select a Topic

There are two ways this may be done. *First,* you may have the privilege of making the decision. If so, you may show ingenuity, creativity, or imagination in your selection. Whatever you do, be sure not to select a big, auspicious topic, one that might also be very weighty and impractical. Choose one that is of interest to you, one that is useful and relevant.

Second, you may be assigned a topic by your professor. If that is the case, make sure you understand the topic, the parameters, and the thrust the professor desires. Since he has made the assignment, it behooves him to see that you have a clear concept of the topic.

After you have settled on the topic, mull it over in your mind for a while. Sooner or later, it will grip you, arouse your interest, and send you on your way with enthusiasm.

Do Preliminary Reading on Your Topic

Select some books which you feel deal directly with your subject. Also secure some periodicals dealing with it. Read these carefully and, if necessary, reread the relevant material until you feel you can reduce the thesis of your topic into a one-sentence theme. The theme will be like the steering wheel of a car, providing proper steering. While reading, gather good reference material, including correct information for your footnotes and bibliography.

It would be a good idea to begin making cards of books you have consulted, cards for any quotation or idea you feel you will use. Cards are so much better than sheets of paper. They are more maneuverable and easier to organize.

Remember, you won't be able to remember all you have read, neither will you be able to recall the book, periodical, or page of the material you want. Don't waste time going back to hunt for something. Nail it down at the beginning.

Now, Proceed to Research Your Topic Adequately

Here are six suggestions which provide you with a good search strategy for your paper.

Consult the appropriate bibliographic guides, which are annotated lists of key reference sources for individual subject areas. The guides are divided into categories such as indexes, bibliographies, encyclopedias, dictionaries, handbooks, special areas, and the like.

Note the call number given for the items in each guide. These call numbers will enable you readily to locate useful sources in the reference section of the library.

Carefully read the annotation for each item in the guide to determine which sources may be helpful for the purpose of your paper.

Look at each of these sources in order to gain a better understanding of its contents.

Using a general encyclopedia or a subject encyclopedia, read a summary article for an overview of your topic. Look for suggested readings at the end of the article. These suggested readings should provide the beginning of a working bibliography.

Consult the card catalog by title or author to determine which books on your working bibliography are in the library.

For additional books, use the Library of Congress Subject Headings to determine appropriate subject headings under which to look in the card catalog, usually in red binding.

Using the same subject headings, consult appropriate periodical indexes. It may be necessary to modify some subject headings, depending on the particular index.

Consult a librarian if you need still more information, or if you need assistance in understanding how to use any source. See that you keep your card file up to date. Also, you may wish to discuss your topic with others or secure outside information through a questionnaire.

Organize Your Research Material

Organize your cards so that they support your main premise—theme—and establish the importance of your topic. Give careful and logical consideration to this organization. Everything should firmly hang together. If you do this well, the writing will follow with much ease.

Outline Your Material

Your outline may follow one of the six approaches to your topic.

The chronological approach, which lists events to be recorded in the order of their occurrence. This is good if the theme is of a historical nature.

The deductive approach. You begin with a general statement and then go on to develop ideas and points which support it. You present evidence to keep undergirding your premise.

The inductive method. This is the approach where you begin with facts and figures, then let those facts, figures, and ideas lead you to a clear conclusion. Your conclusion grows out of the evidence you have presented.

Thematic approach. Here you have an overriding theme; you arrange all parts and cover each with equal emphasis. It is similar to going through rooms filled with antiques. The theme is: "The Glory of Antiques," and you visit each room to study them.

The topical approach. This approach is somewhat similar to the thematic, but it is more restricted and factual, less philosophic. It may be of one word: Louisville, water, food.

The exegetical approach Here you will study the etymological meaning of the words of your topic, their historical context, and the relationship of your topic to the present.

Write Your First Draft (Rough Draft)

Most of the information for a first draft will come from your organized notes which you have arranged in outline form. Leave plenty of space between the lines and also have wide margins for corrections which you will wish to make. You will want to make pertinent comments to provoke further thought. Put those comments in the margins. You may wish to place additional material into your first draft and thus make such a notation where you wish to insert it.

Place your footnotes in the first draft, and place them accurately. Number each footnote thusly: 1., 2., etc., and corresponding numbers should be placed first at the place where the reference is made in the body of the page.

Here is the proper way to register footnotes. After you have placed the number at the place of reference: 1., 2., etc., then place at the bottom of the page:

   1. Bennett, M. E. *College and Life* (New York: McGraw Hill Book Company, 1941), p. 135.

If number 2 is from the same book, do it this way:

   2. Ibid., p. 142.

If there are other footnotes of different authors between the first time you footnoted the reference but you wish to use that reference again, do it this way:

   7. Bennett, *College and Life,* p. 420.

Reread Your Manuscript for Revision for Final Draft

Read your manuscript very critically to see if there is *balance, unity,* and *coherence.* See that all parts hang together in good form and order.

Read carefully to check consistency of *punctuation, capitalization,* and word usage.

Read carefully for *clarification* purposes. Some sentences may be hazy, fuzzy, or disjointed. Ambiguity so easily creeps in. Eliminate all ambiguities.

Read carefully for content quality. Also check to see if your writing flows smoothly and logically.

Now that your rereading has been done, you are about ready to produce your final draft.

Write Your Final Draft

Let your carefully corrected and scrutinized first draft season for a few days. It may then sound different or appear to be slightly tilted or unbalanced. If all the signs are "Go," then write. Hopefully, your completed draft will be typewritten.

Add any appendices of charts, graphs, or tables.

Complete your bibliography in this manner:

> Hamrick, Randall B. *How to Make Good in College.*
>   New York: Association Press, 1941.
> Rorabacher, Louis E. *A Concise Guide to Composition.*
>   2d ed. New York: Harper and Row, 1956.
> Thacker, Thomas A. *Guide for Writing Research Papers.*
>   Louisville: Boyce Bible School, 1983.

Ad infinitum . . . Bless you!

16
Increasing Your Vocabulary

Introduction

The English language is growing, bulging at the seams. The way some people use it has others saying it is a "delightful, delectable *slanguage.*"

There are nearly half a million words in use today with approximately a quarter of a million at the time of Shakespeare. What a growth! But it has been estimated that the average person knows no more than four thousand to five thousand. This is a generous estimate. Add to that fact that the average adult learns fewer than twenty-five new words a year, and, in comparison, it makes the pace of a turtle seem like the speed of a laser. Also, most persons experience little vocabulary growth after the years of the mid-twenties. Most of us overwork some words and misuse others. Here is an illustration of overwork, yet it is a correct usage: "The teacher said that that *that* that that boy used was wrong." (Rephrase the sentence removing the "thats.") We don't need to use a bushel of words to express a cup full of thought.

To illustrate the complexity and interest involved in vocabulary building, here are four examples.

1. *Run.* You know the meaning of the word, but did you know some dictionaries give approximately 200 different meanings? Check your dictionary. (There are 500 frequently used words with 14,000 meanings.)
2. *Piddle.* I am sure you think you know its meaning. Look in your dictionary. Did you know it also means "to urinate"?

3. *Spizzerinctum.* I doubt if you have ever heard of the word. Look it up. You will enjoy using it.

4. *"Accordionated."* Don't look it up. You won't find it. Perhaps it is a word which ought to be used to describe a person who is able to drive a car and refold a road map at the same time.[2]

The Oxford English Dictionary devotes 2,492 pages to the letter *s* alone. Unbelievable!

Words are powerful

Solomon, king of the Israelites of Old Testament days, gave the world a penetrating proverb when he wrote, "A word fitly spoken is like apples of gold in pictures of silver" (Prov. 25:11).

The apostle Paul wrote to the church at Colosse admonishing the members to remember, "Let your speech be alway with grace, seasoned with salt, that ye may know how ye ought to answer every man" (4:6).

So, words should be well chosen, carefully released, and kindly uttered, for words are powerful. Words can sting, pierce, and divide the heart. Words can console, encourage, and inspire the human soul. Words can linger long in the mind and heart after they have been spoken. Words are tools of thought: the inception as well as the expression of thought.

Words are the tools of communication and conversation. They provide the idea to be conveyed and also the channel of communication.

Words can stimulate the passion, the will, and the soul. Words, when carefully chosen, well ordered and powerfully delivered, can cause an army to charge, an audience to applaud, and an athletic team to dig in deeper.

It behooves you and me to give much attention to word study. A limited vocabulary will provide only limited opportunities.

An Inadequate Vocabulary Hinders an Individual

Reading is hampered when words unknown to the reader appear in the reading material. One's rate of reading is slowed comprehension of what is being read is lessened, and pleasure in reading diminishes.

Listening is hampered when there is an inadequate vocabulary on the part of the listener. It is difficult to maintain interest in listening if we cannot understand the words used by the reader or the speaker. Continuity of attention is broken, and the thought is lost.

A *speech* is woefully lacking if the speaker is groping for words or is using ill-chosen words. The power of the speech is greatly halted when weak words sputter and die.

Writing is most difficult when the writer is lacking the words to express the idea or thought he/she wishes to convey. Writing becomes monotonous, drab, and repetitious if the author keeps repeating from the small group of words which comprise his vocabulary.

Skilled scholars are able to express themselves. Top-flight salespersons must be able to make clear the virtues of their objects for sale.

Have you had many experiences when you used the wrong or inadequate word and had to retract what you had said, or say again what you had intended to say the first time? Have you ever grappled for the right word to use at the right time? Have you ever felt you could have done much better if you had been able to express yourself differently and more effectively? If your answers to these three questions are yes, then why not give attention to a program that will help build your vocabulary?

Six Ways to Help You Build Your Vocabulary

Keep a good dictionary close at hand, both at home and when raveling, so you can find the meaning of any word which you do not understand. I would suggest you also purchase a good *thesaurus*—preferably *Roget's Thesaurus*—which will give you *antonyms*—terms of opposite meaning, *synonyms*—words which express essentially the same meaning, and *homonyms*—words which, though entirely distinct in origin and meaning, may sound alike or be spelled alike.

Every student of the Bible will want to have a concordance at hand, so you can locate where words of the Bible appear in the Scriptures.

Give special attention to word roots, prefixes, and suffixes. In this way you will come to see how words are put together. Here are some examples:

Roots

Most of our English words have Greek or Latin roots.
Greek roots

macro (long, large)
  macrocosm—"the great world"
micro (small)
  microcosm—"a little world"
mono (alone, single, one)
  monologue—"speaking alone"
bio (life)
  biology—"the study of life"
  biography—"the history of a life"
geo (earth)
  geology—"a study of the history of earth"
  geography—"the description of the earth"

Latin roots

carn (flesh)
  carnality—"fleshly lust"
  carnivorous—"eating flesh"
loqui (speak, say, tell)
  loquacious—"given to talking"
  (e)loquence—"discourse"

Prefixes

Greek

deca (ten)

Decalogue—"Ten Commandments"
decameter—"ten meters"
di (two)
divide—"separate into two parts"
hyper (exceedingly, beyond the normal)
hypertension—"abnormally high blood pressure"
hypo (under, beneath, down)
hypochondria—"extreme depression"
pro (before in time or position)
prologue—"introduction to discourse"
Latin

bi (two)
biceps—"a muscle having two heads"
bilingual—"ability to speak two languages"
ex (out, out of)
excise—"to remove by cutting out"
en, in (in, into)
enter—"to come into"
introvert—"to turn inward"
pre (before in time or position)
premature—"happening before the usual time"

Suffixes

-able (able or worthy of being)
capable—"able to receive"
-ative (relating to)
cooperative—"acting jointly to same end"
-less (without, unable to be acted on or to act)
worthless—"without value"
-let (small, insignificant)
inlet—"a small stream"
-ship (the art or skill of)
craftsmanship—"learned skills of an artisan"
-ulent (full of)
opulent—"plentifully provided"

Go to the library and find a book with Greek and Latin roots, prefixes, and suffixes. The study of such a book can do much to improve your vocabulary.[2]

(At the end of this chapter you will find listed some of the most commonly used roots, prefixes, and suffixes. These are taken from *Word Building* by Samuel C. Monson. I hope you will buy the book.)[1]

3. Don't gloss over words because you don't know their meanings. Look up such words without delay. If helpful, circle the word and write the meaning in the margin of the book. Better still, make a collection of such words and begin using them immediately.

4. Set yourself a goal regarding the number of new words you wish to learn annually and stick to that goal. What if you learned two new words a week for ten years? That would increase your vocabulary by a thousand words. Your friends will wonder in amazement, and your efficiency level will escalate. I urge you to do it. I have deep regrets that I didn't do it and now find myself the loser.

5. Take a course, if available, on how to increase your storehouse of words. If you can't do better (and it is good) study the section in each month's *Reader's Digest* on "How to Increase Your Word Power." It will work wonders if you will put those words into use.

6. Working crossword puzzles is a good way to step up your understanding of words. Along this line there are available some word-building games.

You can really make the study of words and the building of your vocabulary a lot of fun. Try it, and you will see. Take pride in your vocabulary.

Wendell Johnson once said: "In these worlds of words inside our heads we hold ourselves captive."

17
How to Recite

Introduction

There is a saying, "Classroom recitation just isn't what it used to be." Correct! I can recall during my college days we were asked to stand and recite. The time standing might last ten to fifteen minutes. Now you ask, "Why write on *'How to Recite'* "? My answer is: we are constantly reciting—in response to questions asked, through involvement in conversations, and by the projection of self in the classroom or on the job.

Also, I want to make this chapter twofold in nature: first, to make some comments and suggestions on how to recite efficiently in the classroom and, second, to show how you can write a proposal or a report to be presented to a professor, a governing body, or employer for some project or idea you feel strongly about.

How to Recite

Classroom recitation is a rewarding experience. It is a good way to give facts or to state your opinion on matters you have studied or thought on for some time. There are five elemental procedures in giving an effective classroom recitation.

Come to Class Prepared

Avoid being caught unprepared. You can review the assignment most effectively by rehearsing the gist of the material covered by doing a logical, mental review with books closed. This will fasten it in your mind. It will greatly assist you in responding to ques-

tions covering the assignment. You can't "shoot the bull" in class
without getting blood on your face.

Stand Tall or Sit Up Straight

Standing with an arm on the back of the chair and a foot on one
of the chair rounds indicates uncertainty and uneasiness. A
slouchy position in the chair is a way of saying, "I wish I could
slip silently away from this situation." Give your mind a break by
giving your mind full body support. Stand as if you had come to
attention or sit as if your spine needed stretching. Either action
will alert your mind accordingly.

Speak Up

Avoid mumbling, mouthing, or mashing your words before you
release them. Whatever you say, pronounce your words correctly
and clearly and be concise. Don't speak as if you are uncertain
about whether you want to say what you're saying. You may be
a bit nervous or frightened at the beginning. That is natural. If
such should occur, breathe deeply. Get plenty of oxygen into your
lungs. A good deep breath will also tend to produce relaxation.
Don't hurry and run your sentences together. Keep ample time for
good, deep breathing throughout your recitation.

Look at the Professor

Make eye contact. Your eyes are most expressive. Don't let
them float and oscillate. Don't look down at the floor as a victim
about to be sacrificed on the altar. Make sure you understand the
question. If there is doubt, ask for clarification. Don't be in-
timidated by the professor. Give it your best shot, straight as an
arrow.

Shut Up

When you have answered the question, stop. It is easy to give
the impression that you have a constipation of knowledge and a
diarrhea of words. It is not smart to parade either your knowledge

or ignorance. Enough is enough. If you don't know the answer, say so.

You may wish to offer some thought or fact, even though you have not been asked to do so. If that is the case, and I hope it is frequently, ask for permission to make a comment. It is unwise to offer a correction or an addition to what is being said in an arrogant or haughty manner. Let me give you a tip: if you want to add some comment or to strengthen what has been said, use "also" as your first word. This conveys the idea of helpfulness, not pontification.

How to Write a Proposal or Report for Approval

The time will come sooner than you think when you will need to frame a proposal or report you must present to your professor, governing body, or employer for approval. You may become president of the student body of your college and have jelled on an idea and project that calls for acceptance and funding. If so, don't back away. Go after it. Here are some suggestions.

State Your Case Very Strongly and Clearly

Stress the worthwhileness of your cause, the reason you wish to see it accomplished, and the needs it will meet. Give a history of the situation, your feeling of the present opportunity, and the future value of the project described in your proposal. Gather all the data you can, and describe the functional aspect of your project. You will want to condense the statement of your case into one sentence if possible, but do not cut short your supporting evidence which you have available for those concerned.

Have a Plan for Procedure in Mind

Also, have suggestions and ideas on how to implement your plans. This may call for a step-by-step plan with dates. Leave nothing to chance or doubt, both of which could tend to indicate lack of preparation on your part if you are not careful and thorough.

List the Project's Needs and Opportunities

There must be a genuine reason for it to be. Try to make the need so strong that approval seems unquestionable. Support your statement of needs with all the data, personal support, and anticipated results you can muster.

Have a Budget Plan

If money is involved, and in most every case that will be true, have a proposed cost budget with ways and means to underwrite the cost or to finance the project. This is most important. Have realistic figures. Do not pad the figures or underestimate the cost; both will come back to haunt you. If possible, support your figures with firm bids or reasonable estimates.

List Both Pluses and Minuses

Be honest. Do not try to cover up any problem, and, if and when one exists, tackle it head-on. Make every problem an opportunity.

You Will Need a Timetable

When you wish to begin, when completed, when ready for use. Do this both about the project and the financing.

State Exactly What Action You Wish Taken

Timing Is All-Important

There is such a thing as the psychological moment, the right time. You may wish to open the issue with a conversation. I have found over the years that one appropriate way is to call on your key person and discuss the idea. Have a proposal ready to hand to your friend if you deem it admissable. If you think you may be moving too swiftly, ask if the person would like for you to put in writing the gist of your conversation. This will give you time to incorporate any matter which came out of your discussion. An open discussion will give you some insight into the initial reception you have received, but don't back away. Keep the door always open so that either in person or by mail you can continue your request.

If this sounds like salesmanship, you are right. Everything worthwhile in life has a bit of salesmanship. Education, love, and employment are all areas where salesmanship is involved. The manner in which you dialogue with your professor is a bit of salesmanship. Recitation is likewise. Try to present yourself, your words, your ideas, and your desires to the best of your ability.

Here are three very simple questions to ask yourself after you have recited, presented your proposal, or dialogued with someone.

First, did I do my best? In words, ideas, and speech?

Second, did I consistently keep the attention of the other person?

Third, if I had been on the receiving end, would I have been impressed, convinced, and "sold"?

Learn from each and every time you are called upon to recite, to present a project, or express an idea to a group.

18
How to File and Find

Introduction

It is just as important to know where you have filed something as to have something to file. There are many ways of filing, storing, or stashing away items and information gathered.

In one of W. C. Fields's movies he was shown facing his roll-top desk, taking a sheet of paper from a stack of papers completely covering the top of the desk, and then replacing it further down and deep inside the pile, saying, "This sheet is out of order." It was obvious that no order could possibly be observed.

Another scene showed his method of filing books: "Here are my green books, here are my red books, and these, you see, are my blue books." Color is not a proper filing system.

Squirrels stash away nuts and know where to find them. Dogs bury bones and forget them not. Can we be wiser than they?

What is Filing, and Why Do It?

Filing is an orderly and systematic arrangement of records and important professional and personal information, so they may be quickly and easily found again. Everyone has some sort of filing system. Some use a basket and toss everything therein. Some store things under the bed in various boxes or stick things in various drawers in the house. These are poor ways! Retrieval is almost impossible, and the systems are practically useless.

No one can escape the need to develop some system of filing and finding what has been filed. Important records are coming to the individual in growing numbers. We live in a world of codes, information systems, guarantees, numbers, and paperwork.

Much time is lost brooding over: "Where did I put it?" Frequently, the lack of written, current documentation easily retrievable has cost considerable money. There are usually late-payment charges, sometimes hidden charges, or the misunderstanding of a part of bills, contracts, etc.

Here are some items, affecting each of us, which need to be filed where we can later find them.

Insurance policies
Income tax information and yearly data
Property titles and deeds
Title of car
Bills to be paid
Receipts
Personal will
Appliance guarantees
Contracts
Important personal memos
Birthday, Christmas, and other mailing lists
Loan information
Financial records
Assignments scheduled
Speeches made

(Just a sideline remark here: any financial agreement involving another person should be placed in writing. This is also true of a personal financial commitment or commitments of time and self.)

Usable Information Retrieval Systems

One of the most potentially available systems of storing and retrieving information is the computer. Ours is a computer age. Home computers are now the vogue. A vast number of persons either have personal computers or have access to one. I shall not speak of the merits or demerits of the computer. I am basically ignorant at this point and could not give adequate information. I would strongly urge each one to take a basic course or two in computer programming.

Any young minister who may read this I would refer to the very simple, complete, and functional filing system refined by Dr. David Byrd of the Boyce Bible School of The Southern Baptist Theological Seminary, Louisville, Kentucky. It is called "Byrd's Easy to Use Filing and Indexing System." Information is available at the above location.

Now to some simple systems. At any office supply company and in most book stores you may obtain what is called an accordion file. It is an all-in-one unit with about thirty slots. It opens and closes like an accordion. By putting labels on each slot appropriate information can be stuffed into the slots and can be retrieved fairly easily because the information isn't mixed. Another name for such a file is "The Everyday File and Fast Sorter" by Globe-Weis. These files can be forerunners to more complex and complete systems.

You may choose an alphabetical system, placing information under each title in a file folder or manila envelope. With time, this can become cumbersome. This material may be classified under at least four divisions with each division arranged alphabetically:

By name of individual or corporation
By location
By subject
By date

Another system is the use of card files with pertinent information listed on cards arranged by title, content, or name, and these cards arranged alphabetically, etc.

When the need arises for a complex filing system, then seek advice before taking on a hit-or-miss system. The available systems are too numerous to mention. I am stressing that each individual should start some filing system and continue to refine and enlarge the system as time and needs demand.

Even though we live in the age of computers, supermarkets, and "instant this" and "instant that," retrieval of personal and professional information cannot take place at a smorgasbord line or from supermarket counters that are open all hours of the day and night.

Some Essential Equipment You Will Need

I would suggest a minimum of three, a very basic minimum.

Every person should have a filing cabinet. It does not need to be a four-drawer one. It could be two drawers or even one drawer, but have one type without fail. Let that filing cabinet be the headquarters of personal records, information, and lists.

A small fireproof vault is of great help in storing items which need to be under lock and key. I suggest that contracts, important memos, policies, and so forth, be placed in the vault.

A lockbox at your bank is a good investment. Place in the lockbox items that cannot be reproduced or repurchased. Family heirlooms, items of strong sentimental value and irreplaceable nature, should reside in the lockbox. Lockboxes are the best security possible. I suggest that deeds, titles, and special agreements should likewise go into your lockbox.

Things to Do and Things to Avoid

Some of the Things You Should Do

File or store things properly as soon as possible. Do not let such things accumulate. Become very familiar with your honored procedure. Return them to their resting places as soon as possible.

Keep records available and handy, listing the contents in your vault and lockbox. The mind does forget, at least at times.

If you do not have a filing system, start one today.

Occasionally, review the contents in all your storage areas. Frequency of checking pushes the vision into long-term memory, which can be retrieved.

Some Things Not to Do

Don't be negligent or careless. Treat your filing system with respect.

Don't delay either in beginning a system or in keeping your system up to date.

Don't trust your memory to recall everything. You have a strong memory with great potential, but don't overload it.

Don't hide your filing system. Keep it visible and accessible in an efficient location. The attic is not the place for your filing system.

Don't waste time and money by neglecting your filing opportunities.

Don't file everything. Be selective and judicious.

File efficiently instead of whiling away your time and patience looking for some important bit of information.

May I ask you a few questions?

Where is your income-tax information which you file at the end of the year?

Is the title to your car, the deed to your home, and any appliance guarantee readily available?

Could you provide for me today information as to the breakdown of your charges billed you for your education this semester, the amount paid, and the amount owed?

Do you know where your birth certificate is?

Why not keep a diary? This is an appropriate way to have a chronological record of events, and it will provide memories that are precious and important. Recording of daily events is a commendable activity, especially if and when children come into the family. The best way to keep a diary is to have a certain time each day to record events in it, perhaps the last thing at night or the first thing in the morning. A diary is a simple, yet effective, kind of filing.

Good Luck!

19
How to Increase Your Memory

Introduction

You weren't born with a good memory or a poor memory. Your brain has billions of memory cells and you can store within a few cubic inches more information than you can store in a computer costing millions of dollars. You can take your brain wherever you go—I hope you do—but you can't take such a computer.

Your brain weighs about three pounds and is of gray and white tissue of a gelatinous consistency. It contains about thirty billion neurons, none touching each other, and about five times that many glial cells. It is the major seat of activity for speech, memory, and reasoning. The cells do not reproduce themselves. A person thirty-five and over loses 100,000 neurons each day which are never replaced. But there are enough, don't worry! There are two divisions of the brain; the right and left hemispheres. With right-handed people, the left hemisphere is dominant; with left-handed people, the reverse is true.

The potential for memory is enormous and the resources of the brain have barely been tapped.

What Life Would be Like Without Memory

With no memory—there would be no yesterday. There would be nothing learned. All would need to start from scratch.

With no memory—there would be no knowledge with which to begin a new day. There would be no eating, drinking, or walking capabilities.

With no memory—there would be no capability of speech or knowledge of words; therefore, no way would exist to converse with another or to communicate wishes or warnings.

With no memory—there would be no awareness of relationships: no recognition of each other. There would be a total lack of self-control.

With no memory—life would be at a standstill.

What Life Would Be Like If We Remembered Everything

Forgetting is important. People forget with memory as well as remember with it. The capability of forgetting is like a stream flowing to renew and revitalize itself. The wastebasket needs to be emptied from time to time. There would be utter confusion, dejection, and unhappiness if we remembered all the bad and all the good. It is not so amazing that we forget but that we remember so much.

Four Important Stages of Memory

The Sensory Register

This functions when the eyes, the ears, or other senses see or hear or taste or smell or feel something. The sight, the sound, the taste, the smell, or the feeling registers its distinctive characteristic. Once the eye sees something that object is registered, and so on with the other senses.

"Short-term Memory"

The object seen may be registered as a bird, or a telephone number. It may remain in the short-term memory for a few seconds, never more than about thirty seconds, and then it could go into the "long-term memory" for filing away and later retrieval. The short-term memory is an active memory. Sometimes it is equated to consciousness.

Long-term Memory

This is comprised of billions of bits of information, stacked, filed away, and awaiting the call-up. No one knows how the bits of information are lodged in the brain or what stimuli will bring them up. We know only in part.

Retrieval

The fourth aspect of memory is so important it will be dealt with in the following paragraphs.

How Information is Retrieved from the Mind

Information going into long-term memory should go in with careful placement and recognition. If filed carefully, correctly, and properly, information can be recalled from storage.

Association seems to lie at the heart of memory's abilities and retrieval possibilities. It is wise to tie the new piece of information to some meaningful relationship of prior knowledge.

The brain doesn't tire, but a tired body will interfere with one's capability to retrieve information. Recall is frequently better after a good rest period.

There are retrieval tricks and procedures. Here are two examples.

One day my wife and I were driving along Tennessee Interstate 40 when we saw a sign indicating the turnoff to Jamestown. Shortly thereafter, she began to hum the song from the old TV series, "The Hatfields and the McCoys." "Why did you break forth with that song?" I asked.

"Oh," she said, "my friend Kathleen has a friend in Jamestown whose last name is Hatfield, and when I saw 'Jamestown,' I thought of Hatfield, and the thought of Hatfield brought the song to my mind." *Association.*

Another example. Frequently, we are searching for the name of a friend of years ago. The name won't come forth immediately. Here again, my wife has a trick. She starts calling the letters of the alphabet. When she crosses the letter which begins the last name of the individual, the name will usually leap from the long-term memory. The letter trips the release of the information desired.

There are other cues which can be used. You may wish to come up with your own. Here is a little trick or cue in helping to recall information from the pegs in your long-term memory. If you wish to recall the names of the Great Lakes, just think of the word *homes*. Each of the names of the lakes begins with a letter in the word *homes:* Huron, Ontario, Michigan, Erie, and Superior.

The science of hypnosis which seems to bring forth from the one hypnotized long forgotten bits of information. Electrical shock has been used also, as well as the giving of some medication called "truth serum." However, these are used only in rare and supervised situations.

How May One Develop Memory?

Memory is in some part repetition. Frequent repeating of a name or a fact will anchor it deeply into the mental files of the mind. Rehearsal is important.

If you wish to remember a certain individual's name, try this fourfold procedure.

> Be sure you get the name correctly.
> Repeat the name soon thereafter.
> Use the name several times.
> Write it down to see the spelling and to see it is spelled correctly.

Memory is a reconstructive act. It is like building or repairing something. One thought or idea is placed alongside another, or placed over another. Step by step and bit by bit the information begins to emerge from its storage cells.

Memory is developed through reading.

Memory comes through careful observation, staying alive-eyed.

Memory comes from learning, the addition of facts and ideas.

Memory is strengthened through exercise. It should be used.

Memory should be honored and depended upon. You and I should have confidence in our memory. Trust it.

Cramming, tension, and the use of mental crutches should be avoided.

Some Good Provisions Memory Makes Possible

Memory is a good provider. A growing memory is almost as significant as compound interest in the financial world of investments.

Memory improves reasoning by providing facts and comparisons.

Memory improves judgment skills by making it possible for the mind to recall all facts and events related to the subject under judgment. All functions of the mind are improved through an alert memory.

Memory gives poise to an individual and makes possible preciseness of speech and proper decorum for the occasion. This is true, of course, only if prior information has been placed correctly in the mental files.

Memory provides everyday pleasures. Memory makes it possible for us to remember roses in January. It allows us to relive pleasurable experiences. It is a good thing to sit down in quietness and, through the aid of your mind, take a trip down memory lane.

Memory provides important data so necessary to click off the days. It provides the gauging and evaluating of time. It tells us how long it will take to go from one place to another and what those places are. It prevents accidents by reminding us that a red light means "stop" and a green light means "go."

Memory is a time-saver. It is good to know where we have placed certain things such as, clothes, money, and important information.

A well-stocked memory is a treasure chest out of which we can draw wonderful treasures, that is, provided we have packed it well.

I have a friend in upstate New York who once told me that one of his habits at night after retiring to bed was to recite the poem by Robert Service: "The Cremation of Sam McGee." He said it had a way of relaxing him and bringing on restful sleep.

The capability of the mind is inexhaustible. The mind does not tire. Its capacity is beyond imagination. Its strength is beyond human comprehension. It has been said that the average person knows only one millionth of what he or she is capable of knowing. If that be true, then there is adequate storage space in the mind. Neither the mind nor the space are overworked, overbooked, or overloaded. There is plenty of room to grow and expand. All minds and memories do not function alike. Some have the capability of remembering sounds better than others. Others will recall figures, facts, and faces. Musical, mathematical, and artistic skills and talents abet the mind and memory in those areas. Without being too facetious let me tell you what might be a good memory test: recall all the good things you said about your neighbor. "My mind to me a kingdom is."

20
Improving Your Thinking

Introduction

Can we in America, with the highest standard of living in the world, raise our standard of thinking? It is worth every try. One of the true objects of education is to train one to think clearly and act rightly.

Someone has given us these statistics: five percent of the people really think, ten percent think they think, and the remainder would rather die than think. In other words, a large percentage of persons seems to be allergic to food for thought. They avoid it like a plague.

Could one of the problems be that first-rate minds spend too much time on second- and third-rate ideas and thoughts?

What Is Thinking?

There is no simple definition. Thinking is pushing the mind, stretching it to gather facts, weighing the evidence, and seeking for some pattern of unity.

Thinking, according to Ralph Waldo Emerson, is the hardest task in the world. It requires perspiration before inspiration. It calls upon the mind for endless pursuit of an idea.

Thinking is reflection, meditation, and conjecture.

Thinking is the ability to center one's thoughts upon a problem. It is the capacity to establish some sort of mental procedure with all things considered.

Thinking is the ability to shut out distraction, letting an idea revolve in our minds, and eventually resolve itself. It is patience in allowing a concept or thought to brew as it is being mused over.

Procedural Steps in Thinking

Scientific thought usually follows four stages. *First,* the basic idea(s) needs to be studied meticulously. This includes gathering and evaluating information and carefully scrutinizing all actions and reactions in the rudiments of the problem or intended discovery. *Second,* there is the unconscious mulling over the material gathered. This essentially allows sufficient time for the data to undergo the process of fermentation. *Third,* eventually an answer will become apparent. The resolution may go through several evolutions, requiring additional data and a more in-depth familiarization of the components involved before a final conclusion can be drawn. *Fourth,* the obvious or end result(s) should always be tested.

Most philosophers, psychologists, and educators agree that several steps are essential in any attempt at thinking toward a solution or final conclusion to a situation or problem. *First,* the situation must be analyzed. This requires separating the essential parts and exploring their relationships to each other and to other known facts. The *second* step consists of putting all pertinent information into well-organized order. The *third* requires a thorough and ethical evaluation of all prior work completed. *Fourth,* an interpretation is made of the conclusions deduced through the preceding three steps.

There Are Many Aids to Stimulate Thought

Take Time

One cannot force an idea into birth, nor give thought a caesarean birth. You may need to put some chores aside to have time to think.

There Must Be Exterior and Interior Solitude

Thinking is not done well in the midst of furor, rushed activities, and tight schedules. Solitude provides a great atmosphere for the emergence of thoughts. It clears the "highway" over which thinking must pass freely.

You Think Best About Things Which Interest You

In this respect you must be careful not to allow barnacles of the past to predetermine your thought limitations.

Heighten Your Curiosity

Ask questions. Seek for information and answers. Look under "rocks and stones." Look behind barriers. Climb over fences in order to peer at new ground.

Have a Place and Time Conductive to Thought

Moral Integrity Is Essential to High Thinking

Organize All Data and Facts

Some overall purpose or picture will begin to emerge so that virtue and vices, pluses and minuses, are segregated and not interwoven.

Reflect and Meditate

You can talk too much and think too little. You will think better if you close both your eyes and your mouth.

Be Alert in Your Observations

You may train yourself to see what others may not see. Look for the patterns as well as the aberrations.

Withhold Judgment Until All Facts Are In

Don't jump at conclusions. There is no gold medal given for jumping at conclusions.

Obstacles to Thought

There are many and getting to be more obstacles to thought. We have never been able to weed these out successfully.

Let me list ten of these:

Prejudice and Tradition

Prejudice may be a lazy person's substitute for thinking. Tradition may create mental one-sidedness. You must try to free yourself of prejudice and tradition. It's not an easy thing to do, but keep an open mind.

Obsession with Things

Preoccupation with trivia, will hinder the thought processes.

An Inferiority Complex

If you have already concluded that you are a poor thinker, you may have one, but there is no reason for you to give in, give up, and succumb to a life of living on the ready-made thoughts of others.

Education May Put Strains on You

It can rein in whatever thought training may be occurring.

Self-centeredness

This can deal a hard blow to your thought processes. Don't let your thinking center around "I, Me, and Myself."

Easy Reading

Reading without thinking may be just borrowing another's thoughts.

Physical Conditions

Nervousness, high emotional waves, and fatigue are all enemies of thought.

Failure to Use All Available Information

Remember the familiar illustration of the eighteen-wheel truck which was stuck in the underpass? The truck drivers talked and planned how they might free the vehicle. Along came a lad who suggested they let some air out of the tires. This they did, freeing the truck.

Avoid Mental One-sidedness

Mental ghosts and snap judgments stimulated by past experiences or suggestions of others can be deadly.

Imitation

Don't be a copycat. It can stifle your own originality.

A Dirty Dozen of Distorted Thinking

Earl Ubell wrote an article in the October 7, 1984, issue of *Parade Magazine* titled: "How to Think Clearly,"[1] in which he listed what he called "a dirty dozen of distorted thinking." These may overlap previous statements somewhat. Here they are:

1. *Every:* Called by psychologists as "overgeneralization." This simply means that after one or two instances or events one jumps to the conclusion that it happens everytime and perhaps to everybody, everywhere.

2. *Poisoning the Positive:* This calls in distrust and discourages clearness of mind.

3. *The Shoulds:* Impossibilities are set up for yourself.

4. *All or Nothing:* No in-between for everything is either black or white.

5. *No! No! No!:* Harping on other's actions.

6. *Mind Reading:* Here you think you know the other person's mind.

7. *Catastrophizing:* Here you may view everything as a catastrophe or a crisis. This sort of mental procedure paralyzes action.

8. *I! I! I!:* You are the cause of everything: self-blame.

9. *Mislabeling:* Here you paint a picture not of what exists, but of your own fear or fantasy.

10. *Thoughts as Things:* You make real things out of some things which exist only in your head.

11. *Emotional Reasoning:* This is being guided by your emotions.

12. *Magnify/Minimize:* You either, or both, exaggerate or downplay a situation.

How to Think Your Way Up the Ladder

Think *creatively, imaginatively.* Get out of the rut of usual conventional thought. Set your imagination afire.

Think *positively.* Negative thinking doesn't generate any energy that will provide a breakthrough.

Think *clearly, logically,* and *rationally.* Think in a straight line. Avoid going in circles.

Think *objectively.* Here you want to remove self and look at matters without self-centeredness. Let the facts speak for themselves.

Think *inquisitively,* "why-ly." Ask why, how do you know, and what else does it say and do? Keep on asking.

Think *specifically.* Stay on target. Acting without thinking is like shooting without aiming. Bring your thoughts into focus. Don't let them roam.

Think *broadly.* Get a larger perspective in order to see the center of the idea or thought.

Think *intuitively* and *aggressively,* for ideas and actions may never come around again.

Think *evocatively.* This is the act of calling out or calling from seclusion peaks of the past: extra effort, acts of nobility, high moments of experience, and the memory of early years. Within these are a veritable mine of evocative moods.

A "penny for your thoughts" isn't enough. Thinking is hard. I hope when you feel lost in thought you are not in unfamiliar territory, and thinking is not a new experience for you.

Keep a stream of thoughts flowing in your mind.

21
Reaching Goals in College (and All of Life)

Introduction

It is most astonishing how many persons do not have goals in life. The estimate is as high as 95 percent. A person going nowhere can be sure of reaching his destination. One must know where the goal is before attempting to carry the ball. When the goalposts come down, the game is over and it is too late.

For achievement and success to crown one's effort more is needed than ability, education, and health, as good as they are. There must be goals worthy of attainment. Happenstance won't harmonize our aims nor synchronize our efforts. Dr. Cohen, an eminent New York doctor, once remarked, "The major weakness of our youth today is goallessness." How sad.

Marcus Aurelius, one of the better emperors of Rome and also a noted philosopher of the second century AD, said, "A man's true greatness lies in the consciousness of an honest purpose in life, grounded on a just estimate of himself and everything else, on frequent self-examinations and a steadfast obedience to the rule which he knows to be right." I don't know of a better definition of the importance of goal setting.

Ella Wheeler Wilcox wrote:

> One ship drives east and another drives west
> With the selfsame winds that blow.
> 'Tis the set of sails and not the gales
> Which tells us the way to go.
>
> Like the winds of the sea are the ways of fate,

> As we voyage along through life:
> 'Tis the set of a soul that decides its goal,
> And not the calm or the strife.

So if you and I keep our heads and our hearts (our souls) moving in the right direction, we will not have much to worry about in directing our feet.

I like the Chinese proverb which says, "Raise your sail one foot, and you get ten feet of wind."

What Are Goals?

Aims: These are longings, aspirations, and endeavors toward a point out there in front which beckons onward.

Purpose: This is the reason that provides the energy to reach the point outward and upward. It usually carries some resolution and determination: challenge, a magnificent obsession.

Objectives: These are worthy and relevant components of that something toward which one is moving.

Wishes, wants, and *desires:* These may become a part of one's goals and should not be isolated from the overall plan, nor should they become one's major plan.

Stepping stones: Goals should be achieved by ascending upward, and the planned objective should be reached step by step. Goals are like a ladder. Each round of the ladder is not for parking but for one foot to rest upon while the other foot reaches for the next higher step.

A *spot,* an *area,* a *level of attainment:* Thus these become a journey, a direction taken by one committed to achieve certain things. In summary, goals are "a combination of developed and inherent faculties directed toward external achievement and inner values."[2]

A *dream:* One so thoroughly visualized that there is both immediate and continuous action of the various facets of the dream.

Kinds of Goals

There are at least seven major kinds of goals. They are interwoven. They overlap but each might well have an individual goal.

Academic Goals

Students must either want to just pass their courses, or they wish to reach their academic potential by keeping on, moving upward, ever attempting, and ever achieving. They may set a goal to achieve the highest degree offered in their field of endeavor. This goal would be comprised of many elements.

Financial Goals

You may wish to set a goal which challenges you to have a certain amount of money by age thirty-five. Or you may set a goal to be financially independent by a certain time in your life. You may set a goal to have an annual income after retirement equal to that of your annual earnings before retiring. All are goals you set for yourself.

Professional Goals

You may wish to set an academic goal which will prepare you to reach a certain part of your professional goal. Also, you may set a goal which, if achieved, would bring you to certain levels of attainment.

Physical Goals

You have but one body, and it would be wise for you to think in terms of where you want to be physically at age thirty, forty, fifty, or sixty-five and so forth.

Family Goals

You may wish to plan with your spouse your family life as to number of children, sharing of duties, finances, religious involvements, and your place in society. You will want to plan for leisure time, investments, and retirement goals.

Societal Goals

No person is an island. You should set goals that will challenge you to participate in the betterment of society.

Spiritual Goals

Set goals that will help you mature in your religious faith. These goals should provide opportunities for you to experience your faith in action while increasing your reverence for God and need of Him.

Setting Goals

Whatever you do, set goals that will cause you to stretch, put out, reach up, and develop your potential as you aim higher.

Honestly Evaluate Both Your Strengths and Weaknesses

Take an inventory of your working materials: your talents, likes and dislikes, your inclinations, your interests, and your skills— both honed and untouched. It would have been very foolish for me to have set for myself the goal of becoming an opera singer. I have not the body, voice, nor musical talent. Stay close to what God has given you.

Do Not Set Goals Based on Wishes of Your Parents

Your parents are not you. They cannot choose for you. They can assist, encourage, and help, but that is all. Many persons have accepted goals for their lives from their parents only to learn later that they were on the wrong track.

Set Your Own Goals, but Not from Impressions You Have Gotten from Others

You may have been impressed by the eloquence of an orator, the skilled rhetoric of a lawyer, the glamor of a physician, the beauty of the voice of the singer, and so forth, but none of these may be right for you. Be careful.

Your Goals Should Always Be Aimed High and Far

Keep moving in that direction.

Your Goals Should Be Challenging, Worthwhile and Reachable

Impossible goals are not worthwhile goals. Your goals should be in line with your strengths, aims, and purposes.

It would be foolish of me to say to twenty-four of you that each one can become President of the United States if you set your goal in that direction. Such would be, in the first place, a physical impossibility. Four (four years in office) times twenty-four would be ninety-six and if we add thirty-two (the youngest possible age for a president) to ninety-six, we get 128 years, a chronological impossibility in a lifetime, since each succeeding President would be four years older.

Set goals that are upward, logical, and sensible. They should be big enough, bigger than yourself. Don't be wrapped up in a package of self—that's too small a package. Be sure you know what you want, where you are going, what you have to take with you, and how you intend to get there.

Hindrances in Reaching a Goal

Frustration

As you look at the goal you have set, you may feel it. Remember that a goal wisely set and planned is nothing more than a series of activities, any one of which you can do one at a time. Change frustration into forcefulness.

Conflict

In the midst of your striving, conflicts are inevitable. They come as more and more demands pile upon your time, your talents, and your materials. The strife of the conflict may sharpen your aims, desires, and determination.

Tension

It builds as you push onward and upward. The strain is strenuous. Time crowds upon you. If you have set too short a time period, there is no sin in readjusting your goal's timetable. Don't ditch it!

Some aspect of your goal may well be *inappropriate, unreasonable,* or too high, bringing about initial defeat. We can rise from the prone posture of defeat a stronger person. The initial defeat need not be fatal.

Avoid Carelessness and Indifference

Both are enemies to reaching a goal. Most of the virtue in goal setting comes from the struggle in attempting to reach the goal.

Get Rid of Negative Thoughts

Don't cry, "Fate is against me." Don't feel sorry for yourself.

Helps in Reaching Goals

Here are ten suggestions:

Have a Complete Vision of Your Goals

Know what they are. Believe in them. Select them with wisdom, judgment, and enthusiasm.

Make Careful Plans

Set out a step-by-step procedure with a timetable in hand. Work hard at carrying out your plans.

Discipline Yourself

Stay on the right track. Review your goal and your progress. Evaluate your efforts and achievements. Never build a case against yourself. Don't give yourself the runaround.

Constantly Strive to Improve Yourself

You should pick up steam as you move from level to level. Match improvement with each new height achieved.

Be Willing to Pay the Price

It may call for sacrifice on your and your spouse's part, if you are married. You may not be able to drive a luxury car all the way. You may need to ride the bus or walk. The view at the top is worth the arduous climb.

Be Enthusiastic and Optimistic

Support all of your powers and efforts with inward acclaim and outward drive.

Dare to Be Different

Take a risk. The rate of upward mobility is not always the same for everyone.

Be Ready When Opportunity Knocks

It often knocks only once. Watch for the open door, the circumstance that might be pregnant with possibilities.

Catch the Intellectual Itch

(I hope it isn't just a seven-year itch.) Associate with those who have it, and try to catch it from them. Drawn inspiration from those who have achieved. Scratch and scratch your mind.

Be Truly Sincere and Honest with Yourself and Others

Shortcuts can become lethal uppercuts, flooring you. If your goal is one that will allow you to be less than sincere, honest, and upright, then shuck it and go for another one.

Remember: It has been said what the mind can conceive and believe, it can achieve. Altitude is determined by attitude and aspiration.

Set Lifelong Goals

Once you have tested the excitement, joy, and significance of reaching some of your short-term goals, look toward establishing goals to the end of your journey. Just recall that goals cure boredom, put variety and spice into life, and give one something to live for. Goals make us sensitive to those things at work which affect our efforts toward our goals.

A personal reference: I am over seventy years of age. I have as many and as definite goals as ever. I visualize where I want to be in ten years and I have specific things between now and then that I am determined to accomplish if God but lets me live. I can see myself at work bringing those visualized goals into reality.

My ultimate goal is to spend life to the fullest in service and self-actualization, looking forward to that day when I shall "see God in all His glory and fellowship with Him and His Son and loved ones throughout eternity." That goal was birthed by grace, saving faith, and then followed by works. Isn't it true that our life goals come the same way—faith in ourselves and God, coupled with hard work step by step?

Don't look backward because it may be easier to know where you have been, but look forward, figure out where you want to go, and how you are going to get there.

22
How to Motivate Oneself

Introduction

Questions have been asked and even books written on subjects such as: "What Makes Sammy Run?" and "What Makes Jimmy Tick?" The hypothesis is that some people just seem to have an inner drive or compulsion that spurs them onward and upward. It is a good thing to be able to handle self like the handling of a car: control the steering, provide for and regulate the power, and know when to apply the brakes.

What is Motivation?

Webster's dictionary says *motivation* means to impel, move, incite, and empower one toward an object or a goal.

In sales parlance it means:

Pressing the *hot* button to spark action
Possessing a self-starter and go power
Obeying an inner drive
Shifting at times into overdrive
Practicing spizzerinctum—the ability to get up and go
Acting upon a stimulus
Putting forth second- and third-mile effort and energy
Sticking to the task with enthusiasm

Motivation is having the ability and concentration to go from the plane described in Shakespeare's *Hamlet,* when Hamlet asked the question: "What is man, if his chief good and market of his time be but to sleep and feed?" (Act IV, Scene IV), to the level Hamlet describes in Act II, Scene II: "What a piece of work is a man! how noble in reason! how infinite in faculty! in form and moving how express and admirable! in action how like an angel! in apprehension how like a god! the beauty of the world! the paragon of animals."

How is Motivation Produced?

Samuel Johnson said, "There are two great movers of the human mind: the desire of good and the fear of evil."

Virgil gave his opinion thusly: "The noblest motive is the public good."

Here are twelve things which can produce self-motivation, not listed in priority preference.

Survival

It has always been necessary for the individual to struggle for survival. It has been either—and in some cases, both—that one fights for and adapts self to survive. Humans labor incessantly for food, clothing, and the material things necessary for living and also adapt themselves to the conditions of their environment. The harder one struggles and the wiser one makes the adaptation, the better life becomes.

Fear

This has produced in many people the drive—the stimulus to press self to the limit in order to provide self-protection or safety of family and home—to create a calm and peaceful existence.

Happiness

Most people strive for happiness and pleasure. Happiness, however, is more a state of the mind and soul, and less of the body

Self-expression

"I gotta be me." There is a strong desire in many to see jus what, how far and how well talents, energy, and curiosity can be pushed and developed.

Wealth

We want money. We need money. We want things which money can buy. We want to be able to provide the basic needs and opportunities for ourselves and our families. We may be slightly prone to be a little greedy, but money is important, and the important thing about money is to use it properly.

Service

There is in most persons a spark of altruism, a desire to do some constructive work in life. I have found that deep inside of the average individual is an urge to be helpful. This can become a strong and powerful urge, and it is usually a character trait of the great persons whose names have endured the centuries.

Success

Ambition is a basic ingredient in self-motivation. People want to succeed, to win the race. They would like to hear a commendation of "Well done."

Love

This is one of the strongest of the elements. Love has driven persons to spend all: all of self and all the means of self in trying to achieve a desired end. It has produced a host of martyrs and an array of humanitarians who have blessed the world.

Hate

Just the opposite of love it has driven persons to murder, to stealing, and to horrible vengeance.

Adventure

The call of the wild: desire to fathom the depths of the ocean, to scale the heights of the highest mountains, to soar into the ethereal blue sky, to enter the darkest forest, to probe the tinest cell, to peer into the distant galaxies, and to wrestle with the viruses which affect us have been self-motivation producers.

Freedom

Who is there among us who has not wished for freedom of mind and body: freedom to think and to do? We want room enough to do as we please. (Hopefully, what we please is acceptable to God.) Our desire for freedom goes even to the gate of death and beyond. We want the power to cast off the shackles of death in order to enjoy the afterlife with God and His Son in the place prepared for us.

Desire for Recognition

Do we not respond with renewed energy when we hear expressions of gratitude and comments of appreciation for a job well done?

As a footnote, Richard Cabot wrote a book seventy years ago entitled: *What Men Live By,* in which he expounded his thesis that there are four things driving people onward: work, love, worship, and play.

There are no doubt other solid elements which motivate people, and you just might find a different one for yourself.

How Do You Learn Self-motivation?

Try to take a good look inside yourself. Try to locate the switch, the pedal, and the starter that makes you click and tick. Think of your goals, your time, and your values, then ask yourself if you are willing to pay the price of accomplishment.

Motivation comes from a mind-set. It must eventuate into that. Warren Hilton in volume 1, page 29 of *The Society of Applied Psychology* said, "Your mind is the executive office of this personal corporation, its directing 'head.' Your body is the corporation's 'plant'. Eyes and ears, sight and smell and touch, hands and feet—these are the implements, the equipment."[1] And in volume 12, page 32, "For every idea is a pent-up reservoir of energy, and every idea must find its release in action, and every thought complex has its emotional element, and every harmonized state of consciousness is energizing, purposive and effective."[2]

We must hold ever in our minds our vision, a high purpose in life with unshakable faith in its attainment. The more unwavering is our faith, the more inflexible is our purpose.

Eddie Robinson—football coach at Grambling University who has broken Bear Bryant's record of 323 victories, which includes the records of Alonzo Stagg and Pop Warner—said, "If you challenge failure, you will have the pleasure of success."

Do not waste time wondering if you will succeed. Keep your mental vision sharp and well focused. Have an inflexible purpose and an unshakable faith that will shake off a temporary setback. Concentrate on your efforts to attain.

Practice deliberate persistence, not just mere routine procedure.

Along the way you will be stimulated by results which will come to you and the *rewards* which will accompany the results you have achieved. Some *recognition,* likely, will follow closely the results and rewards. This will add much stimulation, enthusiasm, and new energy.

To those willing to go the second mile, you will find personal therapy is most helpful.

Here are a few therapy suggestions:

> Practice imagineering;
> Practice a sense of humor;
> Practice praying;
> Practice envisioning success;
> Practice use of the words *serenity, success, peace,* and *victory.*

There are four secondary elements which overlap and interweave themselves into the others which I have mentioned:

Curiosity: be inquisitive.

Competence: do everything to the best of your ability—the first time.

Copying: emulate others. Read biographies of the successful.

Commitment: throw yourself into the project without reservation, but with judgment.

The Three *E's* (Enemies) of Motivation

Self-motivation is not automatic like the turning of the ignition key. Once it has gone into telling effectiveness, you must beware of:

Excuitis. It is quite easy for an obstacle or an initial defeat to cause you to produce excuses which may take deep root and grow instantly and injuriously. You might try to explain your defeats or inability to cope with the obstacles by saying, "I didn't do it. Someone else blew it. It's bad, and I can't go on." Wake up! An initial defeat or an obstacle is not insurmountable. Take a realistic look at the failures, and realize they do happen. Identify the culprit: the situation which caused the failure. Rehearse what caused the failure and resolve not to make the same mistake again. Learn from each experience.

Fear of making mistakes. Who doesn't make a mistake here and there? When it happens, assume the blame and shape up your slipups. Don't take yourself too seriously. A mistake honestly made shows you are human. Try to factor out the error factor. Was it fatigue, noise, lack of facts, emotional distress? If it is a memory limitation, use reminders to assist your memory. Please don't fantasize that errors can be totally eliminated, just learn to cope with them successfully.

Extremes. Some people just operate in the extremes. They push beyond their competence level and assume goals that are unrealistic and impractical. Self-motivation doesn't bring out superhuman abilities, talents, and never-ceasing energy. Self-motivation is best operable within the scope of one's realistic goals, abilities, and commitments.

Get started . . . keep going . . . climb higher.

23
Using the Dictionary

Introduction

Outside of the Bible, the dictionary may be the most valuable book in the world for the student. And, like the Bible, it may suffer badly from misuse. One of the best investments you can make as a student is to acquire the best available dictionary. There is an education in the dictionary: it is a small library. Anatole France expressed admiration for the dictionary when he wrote, "It is merely the universe arranged in alphabetical order."

The best means of learning how to use the dictionary is simply to use it—and use it again and again.

What Is the Dictionary?

Most people think the dictionary contains only definitions of words, pronunciations of those words, derivations and spellings of words. But there is far more. Alongside that fact is the assumption people know how to use the dictionary. What a misguided assumption!

Here are the definitions of a dictionary as given in the *American Heritage Dictionary, Second College Edition* and in *Webster's Seventh New Collegiate Dictionary.*

According to the *American Heritage Dictionary,* Second College Edition,[1] a dictionary is:

1. A reference book containing an explanatory alphabetical list of words, either comprehensive or limited to a particular category,

with information given for each word, including meaning, pronunciation, etymology, and often usage guidance.

2. A book listing the words of a language with translations into another language.

3. A book listing words or other linguistic items with specialized information about them: a medical dictionary for example.

Webster's Ninth New Collegiate Dictionary defines a dictionary as:

1. a reference book containing words usually alphabetically arranged along with information about their forms, pronunciation, functions, etymologies, meanings, and syntactical and idiomatic uses.

2. a reference book listing alphabetically terms or names important to a particular subject or activity along with discussion of their meanings and applications.[2]

Compare these two definitions. Notice they are basically the same, yet there is a slight variation between the two. This suggests that it would be a good practice to consult several dictionaries from time to time.

Kinds of Dictionaries

There are many published editions of dictionaries of all shapes and sizes. There are abridged and unabridged dictionaries, juvenile and secondary-school dictionaries, dictionaries of various languages (English, German, French, for example), pocket-size dictionaries, several-volume dictionaries, dictionaries of abbreviations, dictionaries of synonyms, acronyms, and antonyms, dictionaries of dialect and one of American English on historical principles. Then, too, there are special dictionaries like those of medical terms, slang, etc. Most dictionaries are arranged alphabetically and are easy to use.

One type you may not be familiar with is the dictionary of synonyms and antonyms. One of the best on the market is *Roget's Thesaurus of English Words and Phrases.* It operates the reverse from the dictionary. A dictionary gives a listing of words alphabetically, merely explaining the meaning of those words while a thesaurus, given an idea or one-word subject, supplies the word or words by which the idea or subject may be most fitly and aptly expressed.

For example, take the word *new*. It is listed in the index alphabetically, and you will notice it has the following synonyms listed under it as separate references: different, additional, novel, repetition, reproduction, and improvement. Then when you turn to the meaning of "new" as *novel,* you will find many synonyms given. The first section will be nouns followed by verb, adjective, and adverb sections. The word *novel* is listed as # 123 under the caption "newness," and just following it is # 124 with the caption *oldness,* which is the antonym of newness, and the same treatment is given the word *oldness.*

You will find a thesaurus most helpful. Use it frequently.

What are the Basic Contents of a Dictionary?

I will give you a brief digest of the contents of four different dictionaries and then deal with the table of contents of one of these.

The Random House Dictionary of the English Language, the *Unabridged Edition,* which is, of course, published by Random House. It contains 2,025 pages with forty sections such as concise French, Spanish, German, and Italian dictionaries, plus a listing of oceans, seas, lakes, and noted waterfalls of the world. Also given are the major rivers of the world, islands, deserts, volcanoes, and major mountain peaks of the world, all in addition to the meaning of several hundred thousand words.

Webster's Third New International Dictionary of the English Language, unabridged, in two volumes. It states that all experiences and resources of more than one hundred years of Merriam Webster dictionaries are included. There are 2,648 pages in the two volumes published by G. & C. Merriam. There are fifteen sections of contents such as definitions of words, spelling, capitalization, punctuation, guide to pronunciation, and abbreviations. There are sixty-four tables such as Easter dates, ships' bells, terres-

trial and major planets, truth table, and the Morse code. There are
also two plates in color between pages 448 and 449 and six additional full-page illustrations.

American Heritage Dictionary, Second College Edition, published by Houghton Mifflin, containing 1,568 pages. It contains
two-hundred thousand precise definitions of words, twenty-five
thousand new words and meanings, three thousand photographs
and illustrations, and over five thousand short biographies. Additionally, it contains twenty-six special reference material sections
such as chemical elements, color diagrams, taxonomic classifica-
tions, and a table of living organisms.

Probably the most familiar and frequently used is *Webster's
Intercollegiate Dictionary,* unabridged. I have referred to the new
seventh edition. It contains 1,220 pages.

You may never have thought of looking at the table of contents
in your dictionary. You will be surprised at what it encompasses.
I have found the following, and more, in the Seventh Edition of
Webster's Intercollegiate Dictionary which contains 1220 pages.
Some of the contents are: a guide to pronunciation, vocabulary
abbreviations, biographical names, vocabulary of rhymes, spelling, punctuation, capitalization and—would you believe?—above
all a listing of the colleges and universities in the United States and
Canada![3]

Try this on your friend: Ask if he or she knows that the name
of your college or university is listed in the dictionary. I have tried
this on several persons, and the response is always, "I don't think
so." There is far more in the dictionary than one usually realizes.

The index of the dictionary is equally revealing and enlighten-
ing. There are eighty-nine subjects addressed. The range of subjects includes: the Bible, bells, chemical elements, Christian
names, Easter dates, metric system, Morse Code, radio frequency
tables, standard time tables, names of men and women, Zodiac
tables, and the like.[4]

*STOP RIGHT HERE AND NOW AND
TAKE A GOOD, HARD LOOK AT THE*

CONTENTS OF YOUR DICTIONARY:
FROM PAGE 1 TO THE LAST PAGE.

How to Better Use Your Dictionary

Become familiar with it from cover to cover.

Keep it handy at all times. You may wish to secure a pocket-size dictionary and carry it with you.

Be sure that in looking up the meaning of a word you have the right word and the correct spelling.

When you have found the word in your dictionary, study carefully how it is divided into syllables and how it is accented so you will capture the correct pronunciation.

Do not gloss over any word the meaning of which you may not know. Stop then and there to look up the word in your dictionary. Repeat the word and its meaning several times.

Try to fix in your mind the image of the word and its meaning.

As practice for usage, look up the meaning of the following words used in this chapter:

Abridged
Unabridged
Synonyms
Antonyms
Acronyms
Taxonomic
Thesaurus

Use It!

It would be tragic if ignorance of the scope and use of the dictionary continues to prevail.

Invest your money in an up-to-date edition of the finest dictionary you can afford. Invest your time in getting thoroughly acquainted with your newly purchased dictionary.

Keep that dictionary handy. Look in it for particulars as well. Occasionally, just browse through it.

Believe it or not, you can have fun with a dictionary!

24
Improving Spelling

Introduction

Hanging in the back of my mind is the faint recollection of a jingle . . .

> The earth is round, the sky is blue.
> If you can spell that with four letters,
> I'll give you a pair of shoes.

The jingle was not meant to increase your spelling capabilities but to keep your mind on the catch in the jingle. Surely you can spell "that" with four letters!

The ability to spell words correctly is extremely important, and much of our efficiency in spelling is contingent upon hearing and seeing precisely and clearly.

Spelling Is Important

Lord Chesterfield wrote to his son during the eighteenth century, "Mind your diction in whatever language you either write or speak. Contract the habit of correctness and elegance."

Poor spelling can hinder us. As a sophomore in college I was asked to teach for my sister one day when she wasn't feeling well. She taught in a one-room school with all eight classes in the same room. The day I substituted for her is still memorable. As I was leading the fourth-grade spelling lesson, I asked one of the young girls to spell the word *coma*. At that time I was thinking of becoming a physician, and a glance at the fourth word in the second column struck me as being "coma" when actually it was *comma.* The young lady replied, "Sir, that is not in our lesson."

"Yes," I replied, "it is the fourth word in the second column."

"But your sister, Elizabeth, pronounces that *comma.*"

Comma it was, and I have never lived it up or down. For a split second my spelling had gone awry, but the mistake continues to stab me.

Poor spelling can haunt us through the years. Lord Chesterfield wrote in another letter,

> Orthography is so absolutely necessary for a man of letters, or a gentleman, that one false spelling may fix a ridicule upon him for the rest of his life; and I know a man of quality who never recovered the ridicule of having spelled wholesome without the *w.*[1]

What a stigma!

Poor spelling can confuse communications and destroy the effectiveness of the transference of important information. On the other hand, correct spelling is a great asset in writing and communicating orders, instructions, information, and messages.

Spelling is not one of the troubles of childhood or a course of study that we should try to finish by the third or fourth grade.

Two Basic Principles to Help Us Improve Our Spelling

We Learn to Spell by Spelling and Writing the Word

It is a practice exercise. We may learn to spell by observing the word in reading. This is *by sight.*

We Can Learn to Spell Phonetically—That Is, by Sound

The fallacy in this procedure is that when a child learns to spell phonetically, and if it is incorrect, then he must relearn by sight and practice. With only two principles it would appear to be quite easy to learn to spell, but there are nearly half a million words and new ones being added. Then, too, words that are compounded by the addition of prefixes and suffixes do not all follow the same rule. Also, sounds are akin, but the arrangements of the letters aren't the same. Who among us has not, at one time or another, quoted this couplet:

I before *e*
Except after *c,*
Or when sounded as *a*
As in n*ei*ghbor and w*ei*gh

Seven Tricks to Help Us

Edna Furness, in *Spelling for the Millions,* gives seven tricks she garnered from Dell Publishing's *How to Spell it Right* (most helpful where sounds are involved).

1. If a word sounds as if it begins with "s" but doesn't, look for it under "ps" (*psalm, psychology*) or "c" (*cyst, cellar*).
2. If a word sounds as if it begins with "f" but doesn't, turn to "ph" (*phrase, phobia*).
3. If a word sounds as if it begins with "r" but doesn't, try "wr" (*wrench, wrath*).
4. If a word sounds as if it begins with "no" but doesn't, look for it under "gn" (*gnarl, gnaw*), or "kn" (*knoll, knack*), or "pn" (*pneumonia*), or "en" (*enema, energy*).
5. If a word sounds as if it begins with a "k" but doesn't, turn to "c" (*chasm, colic*).
6. If a word sounds as if it begins with "j" but doesn't, try "g" (*gelatin, genial*).
7. If a word sounds as if it begins with "o" but doesn't, go to "en" (*encore, entrée*).

Some Spelling Problems

Here are ten rules from Norman Lewis's *Power with Words* which can be most helpful.[2]

1. What is the rule in words such as *occur, control, prefer,* etc., in knowing whether to double the last letter before adding a suffix?
     If the accent falls on the final syllable, then double the terminal consonant: occurrence, controlling, preferring, or referring.
2. What about *prefer* preference; *refer* reference; etc.? Does the same rule hold? No, because the accent shifts from the last syllable

to the first syllable when the suffix is added: pref'-er-erence, ref'er-ence.

3. What about words like *marvel, travel,* and *conquer?* Here the accent is not on the last syllable and does not shift when the suffix is added; thus there is no doubling of the final consonant: marvel-ing, traveling, and conquering.

4. Shall we double the *t* when a suffix is added to *hit?* Words of one syllable which end in a single consonant, preceded by a single vowel, double the consonant before adding the suffix; hit, hitter; bat, batter.

5. How can one remember to write *ei* or *ie?* Refer back to the jingle—*i* before *e* except after *c,* etc.

6. What about the use of suffixes like *able* and *ous?* After *c* and *g* the *e* is retained: noticeable, outrageous. This rule does not apply if the suffix to be added is *ing.*

7. What about the word *honor?* Is it ever *honour? Our* is a British ending solely. It is found in American spelling only in the word *glamour.*

8. How can one tell if a word ends in *ence* or *ance?* There is no set rule. The best thing to do is to think of another form of the word: abundance—abundant; competence—competent.

9. How about *able* and *ible?* Again no rule is satisfactory. Here again, think of a derived form: accessible—accession; limitable—limitation, etc.

10. How can you tell whether a word ends in *ize, ise,* or *yze?* Only two words in our language end in *yze:* analyze and paralyze. Most end in *ize;* however, a few end in *ise:* advertise, despise, improvise, etc. If in doubt, use *ize.*[3]

You can see by now that I have no wisdom of my own to offer you. The best I can do for you is to share what others have done and give you some rules long in existence.

Important General Methods to Remember

Fred C. Ayer has given nine such methods in *Gateways to Correct Spelling.*[4]

1. Realize that good spelling is important.
2. Assume responsibility for your own progress.

3. Look at words as wholes or in large parts.
4. Focus attention upon spots known to be difficult.
5. Combine vivid sensory impression with aggressive efforts to recall.
6. Combine visualization with pronunciation by syllables.
7. Associate difficult spellings with known forms.
8. Correct all mistakes immediately by fresh study.
9. Review frequently.

If I could be rather presumptuous I would like to suggest that whenever you misspell a word, you either write the correct spelling several times (kid stuff, you say?) or spell it orally to yourself several times, in order to store it in your long-term memory bank.

Several dictionaries have sections on spelling. This is true in most editions of *Webster's New Collegiate Dictionary*. In the seventh edition, which I own, there are forty-three principles with examples given to aid in spelling.

Use your dictionary. It is an indispensable reference book for the speller. By using it you can check the spelling, pronunciation, accentuation, derivation, syllabification, and etymology of words. Use your dictionary!

25
Enhancing Communications Skills

Introduction

Everyone is in the communication business. It is estimated that two thousand messages come to us daily. On an average we pick up only about five hundred. We also are on the sending end of the deal, and that increases the time spent daily in communication.

The first methods in communication, person to person, were the grunts and cries of infants and the baby talk returned by parents. Today we find ourselves in the midst of a highly specialized communication media: radio, television, computers, billboards, neon signs, ad infinitum.

Good, clear communication comes through best, I think, in verbalizing one to another. Rudyard Kipling, the English short-story writer and poet at the turn of the century, was supposedly being paid five shillings for every word he penned, so a sarcastic wag wrote to him, "I enclose five shillings. Please send me one of your words."

Kipling did. "Thanks." That is real communication.

What Do We Mean by Communication?

Communication is getting through to people. It is putting across the message intended and receiving a response to the message. It is a reception of the message. It is transmitting thoughts, ideas, and facts by words, letters, telephone, and signals. It is the imparation, conveyance, or transfer of information, messages, and ideas by any and all methods available.

Brooks R. Faulkner wrote that those messages

Have a kind of cyclical pattern which repeats itself over and over again. They are: (1) what the person intends to say, (2) what the person actually says, (3) what the person is understood to say, (4) what the hearer wants to hear, (5) what the hearer actually hears, (6) what communication and understanding actually takes place after the discourse and exchange.[1]

He went on to say there are four patterns of communication: (1) constructive, (2) dominative, (3) evasive, and (4) explosive. (Note the diagram as reproduced.)[2]

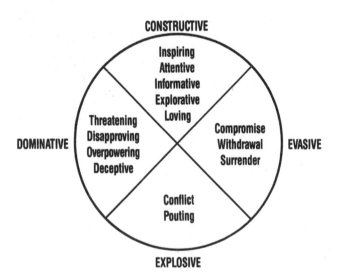

How Do We Communicate?

There are many ways to communicate, such as:

Through Physical Means

Written memorandam: informal communications to preserve information, to inform recipients, and so forth. A written directive.

Letters: these can be exchanged to convey messages and responses.

Phone calls: help to communicate instantly.

Person to person: especially practical because both parties are present, and if there is a need for questions, the answers can be given readily.

Telegrams: good for overnight conveyance.

Telex: helpful for overseas communication.

Commercial carriers: such as Federal Express, UPS, Emery Air Freight, or Purolator. These are especially good means where bulk information is needed.

Auxiliary Communications Support Methods

The primary ones are associated with the individual when person-to-person communications transpire.

The tone of the voice can indicate urgency, sternness, appreciation, or apprehension.

The lifting of an eyebrow can indicate doubt, wonderment, or excitement.

Facial expressions are especially effective tools of communication. One look from my mother if I was misbehaving in public would shuttle a world of truth to me.

Pointing a finger or other gestures can indicate emphasis, give directives, and underscore the importance of a message.

The *seven senses* are excellent communicators:

Touch—conveys quality of texture, sharpness, and content.

Taste—indicates flavor, sweetness or sourness and palatability.

Sight—conveys form, color, identity, and condition.

Hearing—provides identity, seriousness of message, and sender or source of message.

Smell—conveys identity of message and condition (whether rancid or usable.) If smoke, it could convey the burning of a building, something on fire. Burning food is identifiable by smell.

Understanding—through common knowledge and common involvements, two persons can communicate through a general understanding known by each other.

Speech—has been previously referred to as a vital source of communications. Silence can also communicate, usually conveying dissatisfaction or disagreement.

The story is told of a young playwright who gave a special invitation to a highly regarded critic to watch one of his new plays. The critic came to the play but slept through the entire performance.

The playwright was indignant and implored, "How could you sleep when you know how much I wanted your opinion?"

"Young man," quipped the critic, "sleep is an opinion."

Five General Actions of Good Communication

Clarity of expression, either written or vocal. Poor wording, poor writing, and poor delivery seriously hamper communication.

The message must be transmitted from a sender through a medium of expression.

Motivation and desire are essential if the message, idea or thought is to be properly transmitted.

The full and proper reception of that which is being sent is necessary if the intended purpose of the message is consummated.

For the communication to be complete it is vital that some response, feedback, is received. The response may be asking for fuller details, more time or a sharing of ideas.

When Julius Caesar addressed the Roman Senate after defeating Pharnaces II, he addressed the members in laconic dispatch, *"Veni, vidi, vici"* (I came, I saw, I conquered). That was communication at its best.

Aids in Communicating

Brevity is very important. One of the finest commencement addresses ever given was delivered by Winston Churchill when he went back to his alma mater for the occasion. He strode to the platform and spoke five words:

> Never,
> Never,
> Never give up.

And I would be willing to bet you the students never forgot that communication.

Simplicity and *precision* are excellent communication helps. If the communication is unclear and imprecise, then the value of the message has been grossly diminished. Lincoln's Gettysburg address contained only 267 words; the Ten Commandments consume less than one page of the Bible while the matchless Sermon on the Mount has 101 verses. Enough said.

Repetition and *frequency* of expression in simplicity speed up acceptance of communication. Hitler once remarked, "Make it burn; keep it short, and say it often," and people will hear you. (Even if the content of the communication may not be worth hearing!)

The *verbal shock treatment* is sometimes called into action. A college president in Scotland a century ago was being strongly, and in part, falsely criticized by his constituents. Such criticism had overtaken some of his trustees. He responded to the attack with this speech: "They say. What do they say? Let them say." In that he said it all.

It is good to have the *right person* at the right place with the right message at the right time, delivering the message the right way in order to communicate fully and accurately.

Barriers to Good Communication

Don't take for granted that communication occurs. It is not always so.

Don't assume the receiver knows more than he really does, and make the communication too brief. When this happens a second communication is necessary.

Don't assume the receiver knows less than he does and therefore send a lengthy and cumbersome communication. This costs time and words.

Lack of understanding is a barrier. A misunderstood directive can reroute the effort dispensed in response. Make sure all words are understandable to the receiver. There is no place in communicating a message for the sender to parade his knowledge of the dictionary.

Preoccupation is another barrier. My wife has spoken to me many times when my mind was preoccupied, and her message didn't get through to me; it didn't even register. The conditions at both ends of the line need to be right.

Impatience is another barrier. It produces haste on the part of the sender and destroys reception on the part of the receiver. Impatience thus destroys full conveyance of the message.

Some want only to communicate their opinions at the expense of the salient facts. Preconceived opinions and prejudged conclusions stymie the full and easy flow of lines of communication.

When a mother told her son there were three things wrong with his speech, she underscored some barriers in communication. She said, after hearing his speech,

   a.   You read it.

   b.   You didn't read well.

   c.   It wasn't worth reading.

Touché, but true.

26
How to Make Decisions

Introduction

Who among us has not been guilty of saying, "Decisions, decisions, decisions! They come at me all the time. Big ones, little ones: decisions, decisions, decisions"? And they come with regularity and unusual consistency, running the gamut of everything from "Do I eat breakfast?" to decisions involving career changes, marriage, the buying of a home, and developing insurance and savings plans. Decisions are life changing, life shaping, and create conditions surrounding life.

The worst state of all is that of indecision followed by hasty, unthought-through decisions.

Mark McCormack reports in his book *What They Don't Teach You at Harvard Business School* that someone once said,

> When the Ford Motor Company interviews a managerial-level applicant they note whether the potential employee puts salt and pepper on his food before he tastes it, the theory being that such a person is likely to make a decision before knowing all the facts.[1]

I hope that is not the case, but it does illustrate the hastiness and shallowness practiced by some in decision-making.

What Is Decision-Making?

Decision-making is a quality of the mind, the heart, and the will working cooperatively to gather information, weighing and evaluating the facts and figures, resolving what is best through judgment evaluation, and acting upon that premise, all under given circumstances.

There is hardly any way to develop an automatic decision-making process because the second time around all conditions won't be the same as the first time. There are a few exceptions. People who don't smoke, drink alcoholic beverages, or run around on their spouses have made prior decisions of that nature, but temptation still lurks near.

Those are mostly decisions of a negative nature. There are a few in the positive context like: I will work hard, get adequate sleep, exercise properly, and share my means. These overarching decisions are at times interrupted and need adjustment, calling even for new decision making.

Elements in Decision Making

The Personal Element

Most decisions we make will involve some personal aspect of life. They will relate to our capability, involvement, needs, aims, and life's work.

The Material Element

Consideration must be given to the expected cost, the demands of time, the constraint upon our energy, and its place in our priority system.

The Practical Element

Questions such as: Is it of value to me? Does it fit into my purpose in life? Do I need it? Is it an emergency at this time? Can I function acceptably without it? are to be answered.

The Mental Element

The mind must pull out facts, ideas, and past experiences to be placed on the table for consideration. Sometimes a thought will sidetrack progress toward the resolution of an opportunity or habitual action.

A centipede was happy, quite
Until a frog, in fun,
Said, "Which leg comes after which?"
He lay distracted in the ditch,
Considering how to run.   —Anonymous

The mind, however, is most important in decision making. It functions in so many ways as it joins the will in the final stage.

Spiritual and Emotional Elements

Emotional feeling exerts, at times, much pressure upon the mind and soul in decision making. Love, hate, and fear are strong-willed emotions. The spiritual elements of faith, courage, trust, and prayer are also decisive factors. One's relationship to the stewardship given by the Almighty is a vital factor. We all need a place of certitude outside of ourselves.

The Societal Factor

Almost every decision not only affects the maker but it touches others. You and I are participants in society. We live in a certain place and have neighbors. Our actions affect our neighbors.

When a Sunday School teacher said to her class of boys, "We must strive to live for others," one lad raised his hand. He asked the teacher, "Well, what are the others to do?"

The Results Element

How will my decision affect me—hurtfully or helpfully? Will the results be worthwhile? Will the end justify the means?

These seven basic elements are to be dealt with. If overlooked, our decisions will not be well made.

Additional Factors in Decision-Making

There are certain intangibles worthy of consideration.

Courage

Some decisions call for courage and adventure in risk taking to bring the desired results to pass. Without courage and the willingness to take a risk, how would Christopher Columbus ever have ventured forth upon an uncharted sea?

Vision

The ability to see beyond the moment and to dream different, bigger, and better things produces a restless element which must be given attention. Vision may be comprised of insight as well as sight. It may possess imagination, empathy, and inspiration; all have their parts in decision-making.

Optimism

Negative persons are hesitant to make decisions, especially if uncertainty and risk prevail and assured results are lacking.

Faith

It enters strongly into a decision of marriage, spiritual commitments, and those decisions that project themselves into the unknown future.

Perceptivity and Discernment

Things are not always what they seem to be on the surface. Things do not operate in isolation, independently of other involved factors. One must be able to probe under the surface and notice the unnoticeable.

Balanced Judgment

The capability to weigh matters, both pro and con, with equal dexterity and judgment adds extra foresight and skill in arriving at the proper decisions.

I would like to add a few other words. Evaluative skills, "gumption," sensitivity, willingness to make sound assumptions, and timing are all important elements.

Hindrances in Decision Making

There are many, almost too numerous to enumerate.

Fear is a great problem which rears its head all too frequently. There is fear of new problems, new situations, and new involvements. There is fear of what others might think of us when we make our decisions. Fear is debilitating and defeating.

Snap judgment is bad. Haste still makes waste unless one is caught in an emergency time constraint. If that be the case, then action must be taken hurriedly and the consequences are partially assumed by the decision-maker. Snap judgment comes from laziness, restlessness, unwillingness to gather all information needed, and ignorance regarding the issues.

Prejudice, fixed opinions, and tradition put stumbling blocks in paths. Open-mindedness and tolerance can correct much of the negation coming from these elements.

Too much information can cause confusion and stifle one's ability to arrive quickly at the heart of the matter. On the other hand, too little information can keep the heart of the matter covered.

Unwillingness to assume additional responsibility coming out of the decision can thwart the making of a proper decision.

Impatience and impulsiveness are two little devils at work most of the time. They keep asking such questions as: "Why don't you go ahead and make the decision? Making it now is much better." Or, "Isn't the answer obvious?" Sometimes decisions need to smolder, brew, and ripen. They need to age.

Procrastination is most alluring. It is the easy road. Put it off to another day, and maybe someone else will decide for you. Perhaps the answer will come miraculously another day. Perhaps it won't be necessary to make the decision tomorrow. Stall for time, but time marches on!

There is *"the indulgence of reluctance."* This is tricky and deceiving. Reluctance or hesitancy bids for a bit of indulgence. And the time wasted can become crucial.

Shifting the responsibility to others less capable of making the decisions, in order to have scapegoats if something goes wrong, is a ploy used by many. This failure to assume responsibility is both a character weakness and a self-inflicted flaw.

Fence straddling is another hindrance. Trying to play both sides when hard decisions need to be made, in order not to isolate some or irritate others, is weak diplomacy and weaker judgment.

What to Do Once the Decision is Made

Don't try to run away from it. Don't try to dump the implementation on others or into the waste basket. Don't worry over it. Don't cast doubts upon it. Don't try to destroy it if it pinches you.

Once you have made a decision, give it your best effort. Put your part on your shoulder and go forward. If on the way you detect some flaw or weakness, try to take proper and wise means of adjusting the decision or amending it. Decisions are not always perfect but they are starting points as well as involving goal-line stances.

Let the implementation of your decisions reflect your character. Deal with it forthrightly, with integrity and sincerity.

Remember, God gave to each person the wonderful privilege of choice. Choice is decision-making. Choose, decide, and use all your God-given talents in carrying out your choices and decisions.

Unfulfilled decisions are not worth much. Unfortunately, you cannot file them away for a rainy day or a better way. The situation will change, and you will be even back at the starting gate.

Avoid halting between two opinions.

I like the verse in 2 Timothy 1:7 where the apostle Paul tells Timothy, his son in the ministry, "God hath not given us the spirit of fear; but of power, and of love, and of a sound mind."

With backbone, grit, and determination tackle the task. Voltaire was right when he said, "Vacillation is the prominent feature of weakness of character."

27
How to Daydream Successfully

Introduction

Dream, daydream, dream no little dreams. Daydream success-fully. And, when you dream of hitching your wagon to a star, be sure to keep your feet on the ground. Dreamers are the architects of greatness, the makers of empires, the seekers of truth, the miracle workers, the blazers of the trail, and the eternal conquerors.

Columbus dreamed of a new world westward. Washington dreamed of that new world becoming independent of Great Britain. Lincoln dreamed that the independent new nation would make all persons free and independent. Woodrow Wilson dreamed that the whole world could be free. Charles Lindbergh dreamed of blazing new highways across the ocean through airways in the sky. Henry Ford dreamed of a four-wheeled, gasoline-powered vehicle. Madame Curie dreamed of discovering radium. Their dreams were not in vain.

The wisest of men and women have been dreamers. They have dreamed of what they wanted. They have pictured those dreams in their minds and placed those pictures in their hearts, and what they dreamed and pictured eventually came true.

You can't buy a dream, but you can dream.

Kinds of Dreams

There are basically two kinds of dreams.

Nocturnal Invaders of Sleep

Some think these dreams of the night are indigestion-bred. But who among us has not awakened from sleep in a cold sweat due to a dream in which fear of some animal or thing was taunting us? Who has not awakened from sleep just before the dream carried us over a precipice? Who has not felt the cold breath of someone chasing us or the pain of falling down while being chased?

Most night dreams are negative. It has been estimated that 90 percent of our night dreams are in the negative category. The good thing is: most people do not remember their night dreams. These dreams may originate out of psysiological causes such as overeating, indigestion, or stomach disorders. The origin may be psychological or emotional. But we all have night dreams.

Daydreams

These are mostly different from nocturnal dreams. In mentioning daydreams I am referring to those illuminative experiences which lead to new knowledge, often divinely inspired, new commitment, and new courage. These are far more positive.

I want to list several characteristics of daydreams or aspects of the manifestation of these dreams. I am going to run a rather full gamut.

Daydreams have been called by some "quests for the pie in the sky." Some say these dreams urge the dreamer to attempt to build castles in the sky. Such dreams see self going somewhere, doing something, and having something. They push the dreamers to search for El Dorado, the realm of fabulous riches.

Daydreams have been labeled "pipe dreams" as they are unseen and have sprung up out of leisure meditation. They inspire Alice to strive for Wonderland. Fantasizing is a bedfellow of the dreamer.

Daydreams are visions of a Utopia, an imaginary country where one can experience enjoyment of perfection. These dreams are wish improvement, following the gleam of the wishes. "Waves of moonbeams," so they say.

Others label them the call, the lure, or the voice of winds in the mountain peaks.

> Dreamers of dreams! We take the taunt with gladness.
> For God, beyond the years, you see,
> Has brought the things which count with you for madness
> Into the glory of the life to be.[1]

So, whatever you do, don't stop daydreaming.

Kinds of daydreams

Dr. Perry Buffington gave the "top five" daydream categories as:
1. Vocational success,
2. Romance,
3. Money and possessions,
4. Achievement,
5. Physical attractiveness.

Dr. Buffington added that, "in most cases one usually chooses sides and becomes either a 'conquering hero' or a 'suffering martyr.' "[2]

Advantages of Daydreaming

It has been oft said that the measure of a person is determined by the size of his dreams. If that be true, then a person should dream and dream if he desires to grow.

Stephen Collins Foster wrote a lovely song which has endured the years entitled *Beautiful Dreamer,* a call to respond to the beautiful things of life.

Daydreaming is a very beneficial way of cleaning out the cobwebs of one's mind, so the mind is not stifled or covered with nonessential stuff.

Daydreaming has been linked with improvement of mental and emotional health. The dreamer replaces worry with dreams, and action replaces lethargy and despondency.

Daydreaming produces a fantasy life which seems to be well rounded, creative, and pleasurable.

Daydreaming takes the emphasis over the excessive concern of the moment and shifts it toward future goals.

Dreams seem to have a part in the conception and birthing of success.

Daydreams sharpen one's vision and accentuate image production of the future.

Daydreams fuel imagination and drive, providing energy for extra effort.

Daydreaming is a way of putting mind, will, emotion, and aspirations into a coordinated whole which tends to motivate and drive a human being toward the accomplishment of the dream, the vision, the quest for excellence, success, and pleasure.

Ways to Daydream Successfully

If you are to make your daydreams work for you, be sure your dreams are not sleeping joys. You will not be able to build a solid castle in the air unless you put a strong foundation under that castle before you attempt to move in. Castles are not built by oversleeping.

Those daydreams—devices of the mind, part of the basic mental equipment of the personality, and ready-made methods of carrying messages into consciousness—usually spring from material already in the storehouse. The big question is: "How can one take the material already in the storehouse and use it profitably in the workshop of the unconscious and the conscious?"

Walt Disney, who was a topflight daydreamer, once said the secret of making dreams come true may be summarized in four C's. I feel, personally, this would be an oversimplification of a complex, colossal matter. However, the four C's are worth listing:

1. Confidence
2. Courage
3. Constancy
4. Curiosity

Perhaps my ideas are not much better, but I have also grouped my suggestions into four, but with several ancillary parts of each section:

Dream, Spend Time Daydreaming

Dream until you have a clear vision of your dream. Have a bifocal vision, look at the here and now, but also into the future aspect of your dream. After starting your mind pumping, keep it pumping all the time. Never look back. Keep your eyes looking forward, upward, and inward.

Picture Your Dream

See in your mind the quintessential culmination of your daydreams. See it day and night, and don't let the shades of gloom blur your vision. A vision that will venture to victory. Keep that picture, that image, spotlighted. In your mad dash to arrive at the fulfillment of your dream, don't let the image become blurred. Pace yourself so the image is always in clear focus. It doesn't hurt to share your daydream image with others. You will need the help of others, and they will need to see clearly and confidently the picture you have in your mind.

Work Incessantly, Constantly, Honestly, Wisely, and Happily

Associate faith with your daydream and with your efforts. Tie the golden string of faith to your storehouse of materials and your workshop of skills.

> I give you the end of a golden string:
>   Only wind it into a ball,—
> It will lead you in at Heaven's gate,
>   Built in Jerusalem's wall.
>
> —William Blake[3]

If faith without works is dead, works without faith is inadequate. A daydream that isn't worth working for isn't worth as much as a penny for your thoughts. The dream should be big enough to challenge your utmost, attainable only through the use of a strong portion of faith. Let the dream become a magnificent obsession.

Rejoice Along the Road to El Dorado, Utopia, and the Winner's Circle

Stay positive and enthusiastic and find joy in the struggle. Sprinkle your joy with enough gratitude to flavor your struggles. Look upon each adversity and each success as stepping stones toward the finish line.

Remember, the air is cleaner the higher up you go. Your vision is clearer above the clouds.

Don't be afraid to daydream and once you have dreamed, don't be afraid to tackle it with all your might.

Press On

Nothing in the world can take the
  place of persistence.
Talent will not: nothing is more common
  than unsuccessful men with talent.
Genius will not: unrewarded genius is
  almost a proverb.
Education alone will not: the world is
  full of educated derelicts.
Persistence and determination alone
  are omnipotent.

—Anonymous

Edgar Allen Poe wrote:

All that we see or seem
Is but a dream within a dream.

If all of this is but a dream, then let me dream on!

Dream big,
Catch a vision of your dream,
Stay with it,
Make it come true!

28
You and Faith

Introduction

Sometimes it is just faith and faith alone. There is nothing left to fall back on—vision is gone, reason is of no avail, plans are shattered, resources exhausted, and friends have all disappeared. Nothing is left but an indestructible faith, for in the darkest night faith hears a voice, hope sees a star, and love brings forth light.

But in the brightest of days we live by faith. We eat with faith that the food is not contaminated, that it is good for us, and that it is digestible. We sleep in faith. We have faith that we will sleep in safety and awaken from our sleep, that we will not be captured by the dream demon, that our bodies will rebuild and continue to function during our repose. We work in faith. We have faith in our employer, our plans, and the opportunities of the future.

We believe the electricity is there when we flip the light switch. We expect the spark plugs to ignite when we turn the car ignition switch. We have faith there is water in the pipes, air to breathe, and we expect the sun to rise and set, the seasons to continue, the rain to fall, and the stars to shine.

We not only live a life of faith, but we talk much about faith. We speak of having faith, keeping faith, "blind" faith, halfhearted faith, and maturing in faith.

What Is This Thing Called "Faith?"

What Faith Is Not

Faith is not an alternative to action. Work doesn't disappear when faith arises.

Faith is not merely a means of getting some extraneous purpose accomplished.

Faith is not an antidote to fear or a sure cure of the blues.

Faith is not a prop for weak minds and emaciated wills.

Faith is not an emergency light in a dark pit.

Faith is not an extra sense that arouses the other senses.

Faith is not wishful thinking.

Faith is not blind acceptance in default of knowledge, for at times faith outruns knowledge, and occasionally supplies knowledge.

Faith is not in lieu of thought but an extension of thought.

Faith is not a defiance of reason but an ancillary stimulant.

Faith is not putting aside evidence, for it, at times, catalyzes that which produces evidence.

What, Then, Is Faith?

Faith deals mostly with the unseen world of realities and values of the spirit. It is a confident affirmation of the reality of the object of its trust and a belief that it is in real relation to that object.

Faith is a divine resource, an involvement in human lives which makes the fight worth the making. It usually marches at the front of the battalions of progress.

Faith is the venture of the soul, reaching forth for the unknown or the unaccomplished.

It is also the thrust of the mind as it grapples with the unknown, the unbelievable, the undiscovered, and the unachieved.

I see it primarily as:

Belief. Belief is a state of the mind in which reliance is placed in a person, a thing, an idea, or a superior being. It is placing confidence in those things.

Assent. Assent in faith means the acceptance of a thing, a person, an idea, or a supreme being as true. It is bringing all of these closer to the mind, the heart, and the soul. It is placing more weight in all directions.

Trust. Trust in faith is total dependence in someone. It is the willingness to place one's total weight behind the belief.

Commitment. Commitment in faith is the willingness even to deny self in order to follow the demands of faith. It involves both courage and sacrifice. Nothing is held back.

These four may express themselves in scientific faith, which calls for facts or evidence to support its belief, or religious faith, which reaches out into the unknown in search of communion with the unseen God, or theoretical faith, which is addicted to speculative thought.

What Worthy of Personal Faith?

Here are seven things worthy of your faith.

God

Certainly He should come first. It is highly important that you have faith in God as Creator, Ruler, and Sustainer of the universe. If this isn't His world, then whose is it? Even though we may at times refer to the world as a godless world, there is no such thing as a world without God. The world is God's. Your belief in God will bring you, hopefully, to a belief in His Son as the Savior of the world and the Redeemer of sinful humankind. Faith in no God is not faith.

Faith in God should lead you to believe in the personal interest of God through Christ in each human being. It should also lead you to have faith in the Holy Spirit, God's Representative now among us since Christ returned to glory.

Have faith in God!

Others

Faith in other persons is vital. No one is an island. It is not possible to go away from the world. We are in the world and dependent on one another. We need to believe in the helpfulness of others as well as the goodness of God.

Faith in others allows us to cooperate with them in common tasks. It provides cement for society. It causes us to think of our brothers as our brothers and not as ourselves as our brother's keeper.

Have faith in others!

Self

You need to have faith in yourself. Every person should. You are a marvelous creature. You have been beautifully fashioned, greatly endowed, and given abundant resources to work with. You are not alone in this world. You have a Heavenly Father. You are the object of His love. You have His promise of help. You have the special gift of prayer, access to Him who holds a personal interest in you. You have been encouraged to enter boldly into His presence. You have a limitless potential. The sky is not even your limit. You can aspire to the land beyond the sky. Don't discount yourself. Believe in yourself. Trust yourself. Commit yourself to Him and to the higher things of life.

Have faith in yourself!

The Bible

The Bible is the Word of God to humanity. In it you find the road to right living. You can find a blueprint for character development. It is your Guidebook. Believe in it. Trust it. Commit yourself to it. Read it. Study it. It is the holy, inspired Word of God, preserved through the ages for our enlightenment. There is no other Book like it. It is filled with "soul" food.

Have faith in the Bible!

As an American, Have Faith in Your Country

It is not perfect. Many things are wrong with it, but it has provided you the opportunity of an education. It has allowed you a voice in its government. You have freedom of speech; freedom to worship as you choose; freedom to pursue your own choices.

Your every action is not monitored. Neither are your whereabouts always known by the military. Your country is where you can develop your faith in all of the areas I have previously mentioned. Believe in America. Do your part.

Church

The church is a divine institution established by God's Son, Christ, while He was on earth. It is a group of believers in Christ as the Redeemer of the world. It is a place to congregate with others to worship God, to honor Christ, and to learn how to live achieve righteously. In worship, it seeks to bring us face-to-face with God and to send us forth to serve Him in the world. It is His command post. Be a part of it. There is no other organization like it in the world.

Have faith in the church!

Believe in the Future

It is true that the future is unknown, but our religious faith tells us who holds the future. It is in God's hands. Expect greater things to happen in the future than in the past. It is folly of follies to sit down and gloomily anticipate the future. Face it with enthusiasm. With faith in God, your fellow human beings, yourself, and your country, look to the future. That is where you will spend the rest of your life.

Have faith in the future!

How Faith Works

Faith energizes, catalyzes, sensitizes, and sterilizes our minds, wills, and reason in the quest for the unseen, unknown, and unachieved.

When faith is practiced it provides you with something to stand on in life. Life is not aimless. It is rooted and grounded in God. It is a stewardship trust from God and accountable to God. This kind of faith provides a solid foundation.

When fully called upon, faith gives you reasons, ideals, and values to stand up for. You are not a neglected soul with nothing to stand for. Your faith in yourself, others, and your God gives you a reason for living.

Your faith calls upon you to accept God as your partner. He has promised never to leave you or forsake you. He is concerned with your concerns. He is willing to provide the power needed to transform and reform your life.

Faith works without thought of hours. It asks only for assent and acceptance.

How Can One Strengthen Faith?

Since one is not born full grown physically, one is not born full of mature faith. A child's faith expands greatly in the early years. There is room for growth in faith.

Feed Your Faith and Starve Doubt

As faith increases, doubt decreases. Fuel your faith with trust and commitment, and slay doubt.

Use Your Faith or It Will Weaken

Faith unused atrophies and withers. It grows stronger through use. It is accustomed to being used more than eight hours a day, five days a week. It needs no holiday. Stretch it: it won't break.

Couple It with Work So It Isn't Worthless

Faith needs work for fruition, and work needs faith for achievement. One does not void the other. They work in beautiful harmony.

Have Confidence in Faith

Give to your faith more faith. Have confidence in your faith in God. Have confidence in your faith in others. Have confidence in your faith in yourself. There is nothing more reliable than to put your confidence in faith. They work together.

Get the Bifocals of Faith

Let faith interpret the past for you. Let the past increase your faith. The past is not dead. It is still fertile ground for your faith. But also put your faith in the future. Faith will allow you to look both backward and forward at the same time.

Attach Your Faith to the Author of Faith, Jesus Christ

Tie it to Him. Wherever you go and whatever you do, don't break that connection. Let your faith filter through His mind first. It is faith in Him that connects us to the other world. It is faith in Him that brings out the best in each one of us. He somehow refines, renews, and revitalizes us. Faith in Him and power from Him are like two buckets in a well; as one ascends, the other descends.

Faith is not blind. It has eyes to see what natural eyes cannot see. It is not growing weaker, for it is rooted in the Source of power.

Have Faith!

A solid, firm, and self-confident faith helps you to project a personal vision and force that is almost irresistible. It helps you to scale the mountaintops; it has sustained pioneers as they blazed new trails. Faith in self—grounded in Faith in God—can see beyond defeat, trials, and tribulations. With head held high it marches onward. Faith thinks upward and moves ever forward. It generates power, vision, and confidence.

Increase your faith in God,
and
Have confidence in yourself!

29
Upgrading Your Value System

Introduction

Human beings as persons are a free moral agents. They are free to make reasoned value judgments regarding right and wrong in conduct and behavior. They have always functioned as evaluating creatures and have judged the world around them in good-bad categories. Ignoring values assumes that humans are fundamentally nonvaluing, nonethical beings, which they are not. In the earliest of biblical times, when Cain slew his brother, Abel, Cain raised the issue of values when he asked, "Am I my brother's keeper?" (Gen. 4:9).

It is, therefore, highly important that we take a look at our moral and ethical values, a rather complex task.

A Definition of Values

Values can be defined as patterns of choice that guide persons and groups in their quest for ideals or the essences of life. Values are a standard of action as the Ten Commandments, given to Moses by God, were to the Jewish people. Those Commandments have not been repealed. The Sermon on the Mount presents to Christians a standard of action in their pilgrimage toward fulfillment, meaning, and satisfaction. Values are more than ideals or beliefs, for values include a strong, definitive element of commitment. Values may serve as authoritative in personal actions.

The desire to be wealthy, to have a nice home, to be socially accepted, and to be influential are not values but an expression of values. Values assist in character formation by serving as a guide in passing judgment upon what is right and wrong. Values help one to structure, to organize, to order the emotional, spiritual, mental, and physical appeals which determine one's response in a given circumstance. Sooner or later everyone adopts some moral and ethical value system which affects will, conscience, and action.

Kinds of Values

There are many spheres of values in addition to those in the moral realm. There are esthetic values, intellectual values, political values, social, and economic values, to name a few.

Who has not been thrilled by the viewing of Holman Hunt's *The Light of the World,* a painting of Christ with a lantern in hand, knocking on a door, the latch of which is on the inside? Or, who has not been thrilled by a Rembrandt like *The Night Watch,* or a Rubens like *The Descent from the Cross* or *Flight into Egypt?*

Whose mind and soul has not been stirred by Victor Hugo's *Les Miserables,* an epic of a human soul transformed from sin by suffering? Shakespeare, in all of his writing, put no value on the villain, making the villain on every occasion pay for his misdeeds. Boys by the thousands were stirred by the activities of penniless lads in Horatio Alger's books, *Ragged Dick* and *Tattered Tom,* who, by goodness as well as "pluck and luck," reached success.

In the realm of politics I think of the cries of Patrick Henry: "Give me liberty, or give me death!" I think of Abraham Lincoln, who, when viewing the inequities of slavery, said, "If I ever get a chance, I will hit that thing and hit it hard." Or of the late John F. Kennedy who challenged, "Ask not what your country can do for you; ask what you can do for your country."

In the realm of human society one needs only recall the work of Jane Addams at Hull House in Chicago, a social settlement in the slums of the city, as she devoted her life to work among the poor. Or Francis of Assisi, an Italian monk, who disposed of his wealth to devote himself to the service of the poor. Or William E. Gladstone, a British statesman, who guided Parliament to enact measures extending equal educational opportunities to the poorer classes and to pass a bill which extended voting privileges to two million more people.

Consider the field of music and Handel's *Messiah,* the immortal masterpiece. When hearing it for the first time, King George II rose to his feet as the "Hallelujah Chorus" rang out. Who has not been lifted by the great choral work of Johann Sebastian Bach, who wrote the *B Minor Mass* and *Saint John Passion* or Wolfgang Mozart's *Requiem?*

In the field of architecture, one relishes every view of the Arch of Triumph in Paris, Saint Mark's Cathedral in Venice, the classic work of the Parthenon in Athens, and even the modern architecture of the World Trade Towers in New York, or the Sears Tower in Chicago.

It is so true that we live and move in a value-oriented world. We have our religious, moral, ethical, and personal values, as well as those previously mentioned.

Place of Education in Values

Education plays a vital role in value formation, assessment, and evaluation. Of course, there is no umbrella protection under which one can flee when assailed by that which would destroy one's sense of value or values. Education can, however, lay the groundwork, apprise students of our heritage of values, create an awareness of values, and discuss an understanding of the scope and limits of human choices and the need of having a value-related priority system.

Dr. Daniel Aleshire, eminent scholar of Louisville, Kentucky, shared these thoughts in conversation with me.

"Modern education, until quite recently, has been moving toward value-free education. It is beginning to halt that movement, but it still must deal with three philosophies of the last fifty years which have affected any effort to influence moral and ethical valuing of students.

"First, the logical positivists proclaim that nothing can be accepted that cannot be verified empirically. In their views, moral and ethical values are unverifiable and of little value.

"Second, the existentialists emphasize freedom and personal choice to the extent that externally imposed values are untenable.

"Third, cognitive rationality keeps a stance of value neutrality.

"But colleges and universities by their very nature are moral institutions. The institutions deal with aims, desires, choices, judgments, goals, motives, and what the human journey is all about— the quality of human experience."

The core of moral and ethical conscience is the search and reach for something better for self and for others. The realm of meaning and value beyond self is of great importance. Economic aid, medical assistance technology, nuclear waste, environmental contamination and the starving masses all call for value judgment. Education has a role it must not forfeit. With all of literacy, technological advances and noble causes, we have come to the point where at night we bolt our doors and turn on our alarm systems with a feeling of insecurity. Advances morally and ethically have not kept pace with other advances.

Some Ways We Acquire Values

We aren't born moral or immoral. Values are not inherited or packaged as hand-me-downs. Values are not assimilated by learning certain words such as *right* or *wrong, good* or *bad, honesty* or *dishonesty.*

Values are learned through attitudes, habits and ways of judging and acting—in personal transactions with family, peers, or associates. Ethical principles can be learned, emulated, and assessed. Young people need role models, such as parents, professors, or a most-admired personality. Once I had a schoolteacher whom, on seeing for the first time, I thought was the ugliest person I had ever seen. In less than a month I changed in my judgment, and to this day I think she is one of the loveliest persons I have ever known. She taught me polite manners, good speech, a positive attitude toward life, and a love for one and all. My parents were long on honesty and "ingrained" that in me. One of my professors in graduate school had a passion for knowledge along with a personal interest in me. I caught from him the intellectual itch.

Values are acquired through choices, experiences, and judgments. I learned obedience and respect for parents the hard way—through the seat of my pants. I learned the value of money during the depression days when I signed up for something that was delivered, but then I really didn't want. I had to pay the full price: $125.00 out of a $50.00 a month salary.

We can learn from history about the victories we ourselves did not win but have enjoyed: lessons of liberty, justice, and peace.

Peer pressures can either destroy or edify our value judgments. For fear of not being accepted by the group we can surrender our values and go along with the crowd. I have seen the opposite happen; that is, bringing one into a peer group whose life did not "jibe" with the ideals and commitments of the group, but who later adopted the group's attitude and sense of helpfulness and commitment.

Religious commitment is most formative in establishing values. The teachings of Jesus are binding upon His followers. The Sermon on the Mount offers much food for thought and direction for personal action.

Some educational institutions have moral and ethical valuing courses. Courses in ethics, religious morality, and personal development are all good.

Living up to one's own best self is a good way to establish value priorities. One cannot deal lightly with self if one desires to develop self to the fullest. Just as cheap, shoddy material is unacceptable in building a home, so it is with building a life. Things which poison the mind, defile the body, and hurt others damage the individual even more and should be abolished.

> This above all: to thine own self be true,
> And it must follow, as the night the day,
> Thou canst not then be false to any man.[1]
>
> —Shakespeare, *Hamlet*
> Act I, Sc. iii

Things Which Affect Our Values, Value Formation

Values are not easily formed, adopted or accepted. They must be thought out, wrought out and lived out. Multiple factors enter into value assessment, awareness, and adoption.

Affluence Is Hurting Us

We seem to be slouching on a couch searching for a soul. We think a peace economy is an affluent, pleasurable economy. It is difficult to share affluence since affluence has become a way of life, calling for additional affluence.

A Paucity of Constructive Ideas

We are working not at the source of the stream but at the contaminated pool formed later from the stream. We have government subsidies, rehabilitation programs—and they are good, but not sufficient—for they don't teach industry, self-reliance, and independence. There is a sort of helplessness pervading our society: "The budget can't be balanced, the poor we have with us always, and there just isn't anything one can do." But there is more than pessimism in this world. There are optimists, intelligent persons, great thinkers, and tremendous resources.

Rapid Change

Coming with such terrific force, change is forcing us all to take a look at things once not even in existence. Technological advances, in some cases the technology, may be something less than an advance and produce first-time situations where value judgment is desperately needed.

An Air of Indifference

"Well, let me do as I please and 'let the devil take the hindmost.' " This has produced lethargy, a closing of one's eyes to the facts. The force of evil is powerful, and fear has become a part of our judgment.

A Surrender to What Is Plausible or Popular

"It is hard to buck the trend." Or one will say, "Better jump on the bandwagon, or you will be left on the side road." Weak knees never supported a strong back.

A Decline in the Effect of Religion on Public Moral Values

Where once the Bible, God's Word, was respected, and its teachings followed, that is not the practice in the majority of actions of our society. Religious precepts and teachings are worthy of reconsideration to be reestablished and revered.

Sovereignty of the Laboratory is Taking Over

Liberal arts, a great teacher of values, judgment and reasoning are more tolerated than pursued. Questions about purpose and the making of a good life now seem sentimental and old fashioned. Too bad.

Our Relationship with God Affects Our Value System

To be in good fellowship with God, one must obey God and do His commandments. Human beings are stewards of that which God gives to them. This stewardship when properly considered will establish an awareness of value priorities.

Additional Self-steps in Establishing Values

Study, read, think, and *reason* in order to become aware of values, value systems, and standards.

Before there is an adoption of values, *consider the alternatives.*

Once there is an awareness of values, then *judgments are to be made* as to what values and aspects of values are worthy of adoption.

In the adoption of values *it is imperative that a positive affirmation be made* of those values and a personal acceptance in one's life and commitment of one's life in living out those values. The affirmation is related to life and not held as just a theory.

Repetition of the affirmation, acceptance, and the practice in life strengthen one's holding on to one's values.

Never settle for second-rate values or the second best. Reach toward the highest self, the stars. There is value here for your value system.

30
You and Your Miraculous Potential

Introduction

You are a miraculous individual. You have great potential. You are very special. I want to tell you about yourself. When God created man and woman, He made the best man and the best woman that could be made—the best He could make, and no one was there to do better. He could not have done better, for He never acted less than His best. As a child of your parents, you are an offspring of those wonderful creatures God created and gave the power of reproduction to according to the law of like producing like.

You are, therefore, not an orphan of the apes;

You are not a bit of dancing dirt coming from nowhere and going nowhither;

You are not an animal but a child of God;

You are not a forked radish on a sick planet;

You are not owner of anything, just a steward;

You are wonderfully made, greatly endowed, and lovingly blessed.

Take a good look at yourself.

You Are a Superb Person Physically

No animal is superior to you. No machine man ever created can touch the hem of your garment. Your body is something.

Look at Your Hands

You can use them to type, play a piano, write love notes, caress your child, catch a ball, close into a fist, feed yourself, grip a tennis racquet, or perform a delicate surgical operation, and so forth. No mechanical hand has ever been made that is as pliable and as efficient. The skin on the palm of your hand is different from that on the back so that you grip things. If that skin is cut or snagged, it will repair itself. Did your car fender ever voluntarily repair itself? The blood you shed throws off waste and purifies itself and will automatically coagulate to stop its flow.

Look at Your Ears

A piano has eighty-eight keys. Your ears have fifteen-hundred keys. They are so sensitive that in a completely soundproofed room you can actually hear the blood flowing through your vessels. As you hear things with the aid of memory and your mind, you can identify them. You know the voices of your loved ones, the toot of a car horn, and the rumbling of thunder. What protection your ears provide!

Think About Your Heart

The heart is not a big organ, but it will beat 103,689 times in every twenty-four hours, resting one fourth of the time. It will provide the power to pump your blood 168 million miles per day. Its rate increases as your activity demands more strength and power.

Your Eyes

They are connected to your brain by three-hundred thousand separate and private telephone lines. When we look at a juicy steak, thousands of separate messages are sent to the brain telling of the anticipated taste, the color, the shape, and its kind. Your eyes will make about seventy-four thousand color pictures for you each day.

But Your Mind, Oh, Your Mind

Located in the brain is a thermostat with its own nervous system contacting every part of the body. If part of your body gets too hot or too cold, signals are sent to the control center, and blood vessels of the skin contract or enlarge to give off more or less heat. The human brain contains ten million nerve cells. You may exercise each one if you choose. (More later about the mind.)

Space will not permit us to discuss your glands, your bones, your muscles, your nerves, and your blood, all so vital and just as marvelous.

What a body! But there is more. You are the only creature that walks upright. You are the only creature that saves up food for others. You can laugh, talk, and sing.

Chemically, you may not be worth more than five to ten dollars, but your energy potential and mental capabilities make you capable of being worth billions.

You Are an Unusual Creature, Mentally

You can think, reason, and evaluate. Your actions are not merely the results of instinct. With your mind you think of the past, enjoy the present, and plan for the future, yet you cannot transport your body back into the past nor project it into the future. You are a victim of time and space, yet with your mind you can transcend time and space. You can rationalize and decide. You can choose and support your choices.

Your power of memory is tremendous. You have both short- and long-term memories. Through association, the power of recall, and proper stimulation, you can bring forth from your mental storage house forms, facts, and faces.

You can take separate bits of information and place them into logical and sequential form and resolve problems. You can draw blueprints of buildings in your imagination, transfer those thoughts onto paper, and then proceed to build buildings.

Your mind is curious. You ask questions about things and proceed to ferret out the meaning of those things. You wonder about the starry skies and proceed to explore the heavenly host, even building machines that will take some to the moon. You look through your designed telescopes and see more than any naked eye ever saw.

You wonder about small things, and you take your own designed and manufactured microscopes to look at those small cells and little things which the eye cannot fathom.

You desire personal things and set your mind on the acquisition of those things, using your multiple talents and skills supported by your boundless energy.

You Are More than Body and Mind; You Are a Soul

God in His last creative act breathed into man and woman the breath of life, and man and woman became living souls. One of the greatest of all mysteries is the union of soul and body, the interaction of the two. In this respect you are a sensitive and unbelievably complex individual. As an individual, you are different from any other person.

You know love and hate in ways different from any other creature. Your understanding of love comes from God who is love. You, as a living soul, are the object of God's love. Think of what it means to be the object of God's love, to hold the love of God who wishes no good thing withheld from you. His love for you is so deep and eternal that He provided for your every need. His resources are adequate. He gave His Son to redeem you. His grace abounds; His mercy is tender and forgiving.

Not only are you the object of God's love, but He sent His Spirit to guide you into truth, to be a Comforter, and to empower you. He has not left you alone to fend for yourself in this world. He has promised to "never leave thee, nor forsake thee" (Heb. 13:5).

In His Book He has given us a Model Prayer and has encouraged us all to call upon Him and to come boldly into His presence. He has given us the special privilege of prayer and has promised not to turn a deaf ear to His children. The rates have never been increased: an humble and a contrite heart.

His love, concern, and blessings go even into eternity. His Son has gone to prepare the way, to prepare a place for you. A human alone is special as a physical creature of His creative acts, but those who are in step with God are extra and eternally special. As spiritual beings they stand alone with heaven reserved for them.

Then, Don't Think Lightly of Yourself

Let me quote again from Shakespeare:

> What a piece of work is man! how noble in reason!
> how infinite in faculty! in form and moving how
> express and admirable! in action how like an angel!
> in apprehension how like a god! the beauty of the
> world! the paragon of animals![2]
>
> —*Hamlet*, Act II, Sc. *ii*

You have your faculties. You have your talents. You have your great endowment. You have a wonderful body. You are the object of God's love. Pity yourself? No, that is out of the question. Be satisfied with mediocrity? No, you can bump the stars, so why be satisfied with less.

Even though you may have some physical handicap, does that automatically mean defeat? No. Some of the world's greatest persons have used their handicaps to achieve far beyond expectations. Think of Charles Steinmetz, the electrical genius, and Franklin D. Roosevelt, a polio victim, who was the longest-serving president of our country.

You may be less than multitalented, but is that a reason to become passive and despondent? No! Develop that one talent; hone and polish it better than anyone else. Your body will respond. Push it, but take care of it. Your mind is alert and ready to act. Fill it with important facts, ideas, and ideals. Keep trash out of it. Your soul is your great helper, and it will; it will work with your body.

Don't sit down and wait for your ship to come in loaded. Load your own ship with your own hands, and send it out to represent you in service for God and others. Keep your chin up, your spirits high, and your attitude optimistic and positive. Fill "the unforgiving minute with sixty seconds worth of distance run." Take a good deep breath. Feel your lungs responding. Look at a sunset and thank God for your eyes. Listen to a thrilling sonata and rejoice that your hearing is good. Walk around the block and be glad that you can move. Think of your blessings and live gratefully.

How to Use the Miraculous You

The previous chapters have indicated many ways of using your wonderful body, your great mind, your special talents, and your God-given blessings. Orchestrate your virtues.

Harmonize your energies,
Evaluate your priorities,
Synchronize your aims and purposes,
Sensitize your spiritual desires,
Organize your moral/ethical values.

Choose to:

Love
Laugh
Pray
Give
Live
Grow

Avoid:

Self-depreciation
Hypersensitivity
Resentment of the authority of others
Lack of self-control
Lack of courage and faith
Unwillingness to evaluate self
The sin of ingratitude

One great philosopher, Abraham Maslow, in studying leading personalities found these common traits in each:

Purposeful	Spontaneous
Realistic	Self-discipline
Creative	Ethical
Humble	Courageous
Considerate	Self-confidence

You have the resources, the power within you, and the potential to achieve.

It is up to you, but you can have God's help also. Take your choice. Make your choices. Go to it, and the miraculous you can do miraculous things.

Here are two illustrations: First, as I wrote this chapter, I did so in an hour and forty-five minutes, remaining at my old, trusty typewriter the entire time. My hands hit the keys as my mind dictated the expressions of my thoughts. I read what I was writing as I was writing to see what errors I was making. From time to time my mind rushed out and brought in additional facts. My heart continued its regular beat while the food I had eaten during the day was being transformed into energy to keep my fingers pecking away while my mind, body and eyes were performing their specific roles.

The second and better illustration is that which transpired just before I came to my office. I sat before the television screen listening to then-President Reagan. He spoke of his upcoming summit meeting with Mr. Gorbachev of the USSR. I watched our president. He spoke every word distinctly. His eyes expressed pathos, concern, love and hope. He gestured with his hands to stress a point. You could detect that at times his mind was outracing his speech to bring to him additional, pertinent thoughts. He may have been reading from a tele-prompter, but his eyes pierced the screen and met my eyes. His mind, what a machine, operating so efficiently. His body, "fearfully and wonderfully made," was operating smoothly and beautifully. He was positive, motivated and impressive. I thought, *What is a man?* So marvelous and wonderful that he could perform as he did.

You are a Marvelous Person, too. You are a Rarity.

I have been inspired and influenced in writing this chapter by Og Mandino's book, *The Greatest Miracle in the World,* especially chapter 9, "The God Memorandum," which I have read and re-read many, many times.

Notes

Chapter One

1. Harry and Bonaro Overstreet, *The Mind Alive* (New York: W. W. Norton and Company, Inc., 1964), p. 58.

Chapter Two

1. Henry Wadsworth Longfellow, *Complete Poetical Works* (Boston: Houghton Mifflin Company, 1920), p. 187.

Chapter Three

1. Bell, Burkhardt, and Lawhead, *Introduction to College Life* (Boston: Houghton Mifflin Company, 1962), pp. 12, 14-16.

Chapter Six

1. Rufus M. Jones, *New Eyes for Invisibles* (New York: The Macmillan Company, 1943), p. 11.
2. Harry and Bonaro Overstreet, *The Mind Alive* (New York: W. W. Norton and Company, Inc., 1954), pp. 228-230.

Chapter Seven

1. Francis Bacon, "Of Studies," quoted in *Great Treasury of Western Thought,* eds. Mortimer J. Adler and Charles Van Doren, (New York: R. R. Bowker Company, 1977), pp. 2, 16-17.
2. Edward B. Lindaman, *Space: a New Direction for Mankind* (New York, Evanston, and London: Harper and Row, Publishers, 1969), p. 71.

Chapter Eight

1. Edward Hersey Rickards, "A Wise Old Owl," quoted in *Familiar Quotations* (Boston: Little, Brown and Company, 1940), p. 836.

Chapter Nine

1. Elwood N. Chapman, *College Survival* (Chicago: Science Research Associates, Inc., 1974), p. 86.

Chapter Ten

1. Brooks R. Faulkner, *Getting on Top of Your Work* (Nashville: Convention Press, 1973), pp. 133-134. Used by permission.

Chapter Twelve

1. Harry Shaw, *Thirty Ways to Improve Your Grades* (New York: McGraw-Hill Publishers, 1976), n.p.n.

Chapter Thirteen

1. The sample cards and much other information in this chapter were generously supplied by Mr. Howard Gallimore, Manager, Dargan Research Library, Baptist Sunday School Board, Nashville, Tennessee.
2. *Outline of the Library of Congress Classification* (Washington, D.C., U. S. Government Printing Office, 1970), n.p.n.
3. *E. C. Dargan Research Library Manual* (Nashville: Sunday School Board of the Southern Baptist Convention, 1987), p. 15.
4. Information on library automation was supplied by Dr. Ernest Heard, Professor of Library Science and Director of the Williams Library, Belmont College, Nashville, Tennessee.

Chapter Sixteen

1. Rich Hall and Friends, "Sniglets," quoted in *Reader's Digest*, June, 1985, p. 109.
2. The roots, prefixes, and suffixes were taken from Samuel C. Monson, *Word Building* (New York: no publisher given, 1968), pp. 143-151.

Chapter Twenty

1. Earl Ubell, "How to Think Clearly," *Parade*, Oct. 7, 1984, pp. 12, 14-15. Permission requested.

Chapter Twenty-one

1. Ella Wheeler Wilcox, "Winds of Fate," quoted in John Bartlett, *Familiar Quotations*, Fifteenth Ed. ed. Emily Morison Beck, (Boston: Little, Brown and Company, 1980), p. 669.
2. Mortimer M. Meyer, "The Development of Healthy and Unhealthy Goal Setting," *The Course of Human Life*, eds. Charlotte Buhler and Fred Massarik (New York: Springer Publishing Company, Inc., n.d.), p. 189.

Chapter Twenty-two

1. Warren Hilton, *The Society of Applied Psychology* (New York and London, 1919), Vol 1, p. 29

2. Hilton, *The Society of Applied Psychology* (New York and London, 1920), Vol 12, p. 32.

Chapter Twenty-three

1. *The American Heritage Dictionary,* Second College Edition (Boston: Houghton Mifflin Company, 1982), p. 394.

2. *Webster's Ninth New Collegiate Dictionary* (Springfield, Mass.: G. & C. Merriam Company, 1984), p. 352.

3. *Webster's Intercollegiate Dictionary* (Springfield, Mass.: G. & C. Merriam Company, n.d.), p. 3*a*, "Contents."

4. *Ibid.*, p. 1221, "Index."

Chapter Twenty-four

1. Edna L. Furness, *Spelling for the Millions* (Nashville: Thomas Nelson, Inc., 1977), p. 18.

2. Norman Lewis, *Power with Words* (New York: Thomas Y. Crowell, 1966), pp. 311-317.

3. *Ibid.*

4. Fred C. Ayer, *Gateways to Correct Spelling* (Austin, Texas: The Steck Company, 1946), p. X.

Chapter Twenty-five

1. Brooks R. Faulkner, *Getting on Top of Your Work* (Nashville: Convention Press, 1973), p. 67.

2. *Ibid.*, p. 85.

Chapter Twenty-six

1. Mark H. McCormack, *What They Don't Teach You at Harvard Business School* (New York: Bantam Books, 1984), p. 231

Chapter Twenty-seven

1. Achmed Abdullah and T. Compton Parkenham, *Dreamers of Empire* (Freeport, N.Y.: Books for Libraries Press, 1968), Foreword.

2. Perry W. Buffington, "Daydreams: More than Pipe Dreams?" *Sky,* Jan. 1985, p. 101.

3. William Blake, "Jerusalem," preface to Chapter 4, quoted in John Bartlett, *Familiar Quotations,* ed. Christopher Morley (Boston: Little, Brown and Company, 1940), p. 281.

Chapter Thirty

1. William Shakespeare, *Hamlet,* Act I, Scene iii, quoted in John Bartlett, *Familiar Quotations* ed. Emily Morison Beck (Boston: Little, Brown & Company, 1980), p. 219.

2. *Ibid.* p. 220.